EXPANDED & UPDATED

Paleo Bread

GLUTEN-FREE, GRAIN-FREE, PALEO-FRIENDLY BREAD BREAD RECIPES

Rockridge Press

TABLE OF CONTENTS

Chapter 4: Flatbreads, Rolls, Muffins, and Pizza Dough 85

*Without wishing in the slightest
degree to disparage the skill
and labour of breadmakers by
trade, truth compels us to assert
our conviction of the superior
wholesomeness of bread made in our
own homes.*

—Eliza Acton

INTRODUCTION

Is the food you eat making you healthy, or is it wreaking havoc on your body? Cardiovascular disease, type 2 diabetes, cancer, and obesity are reaching epidemic proportions in the population, and countless people also have issues with their digestion, from simple discomfort and gas to celiac disease and irritable bowel syndrome. The solution to many of these issues can be found right there on your plate. More and more medical professionals are asserting that taking control of your health can be as simple as considering a diet change such as living the Paleo diet. This plan has gained a great deal of popularity, but there are still many misconceptions about what Paleo actually means on a daily basis. It is thought to be incredibly restrictive, but as you'll learn in this book, this is not the case at all.

The Paleo diet is not the only eating strategy that advocates avoiding wheat, processed food, sugar, and calories devoid of nutrition. Most mainstream health professionals would recommend exactly the same choices for vibrant health. It seems only logical that cutting out damaging ingredients and foods will make you feel better, make you look better, and cut your risk of developing disease; however, the actual problem with all this smart advice is that it is very difficult for most people to change ingrained eating habits. The Western diet is absolutely overflowing with ingredients that are known to make people sick. Think about a regular day, and you will see bagels covered in fattening cream cheese, sugary cereal, oil-drenched French fries, and nary a vegetable or fruit anywhere! This parade of artery-clogging weight-gain-inducing meals is often interspersed with sugary cookies and baked snacks. We are literally eating ourselves to death.

The Paleo diet is not meant to be a punishment and deprivation of all your favorite tasty treats such as bread and cinnamon rolls. In fact, it includes countless delicious foods such as chicken, beef, fish, eggs, vegetables, and fruit along with healthy oils and nuts. You might not be able to indulge in a honey-glazed cruller when eating Paleo, but you certainly do not have to give up tempting baked products and breads forever. By using nut flours, healthy fats, and natural sugars, you will be able to wrap your chicken breast in a tortilla and enjoy a crunchy piece of toast for breakfast. Paleo breads are delicious, easy to prepare, and best of all, good for you.

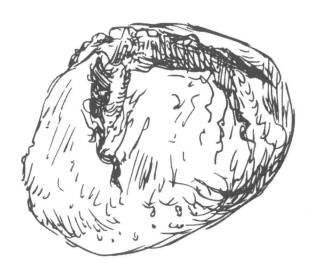

If thou tasteth a crust of bread, thou tasteth all the stars and all the heavens.

—Robert Browning

1

10 TIPS FOR PALEO BAKING

Many people fall off the Paleo diet wagon because they miss bread—simple, yummy bread. There is something decadent about a crusty, warm slice of bread, fragrant and slathered with creamy butter. This culinary experience is possible because of the gluten in wheat flour. Gluten does not actually cause bread to rise; rather, it builds a crisscross protein network that creates elasticity in the dough. This network also traps gas and prevents it from escaping while the bread bakes, which produces those lovely airy pockets in the loaves and buns. A lack of gluten in nut flours is the reason most people find Paleo breads less fluffy and airy. Here are a few things to consider when baking Paleo breads so that the experience is satisfying and successful:

#1 Remember that Paleo bread is definitely not traditional bread in texture, taste, or even shelf life. Don't despair, however—you will still be able to slice it for sandwiches, dip it in soups, and have lovely toast in the morning. Many Paleo breads are actually quick breads, so expect a certain denseness and lack of crust. Try to embrace the unique qualities of Paleo breads without comparing them to their wheat-based counterparts. You will be able to produce some truly delicious bread using Paleo recipes, but as with regular baking, not every attempt will be a success. Be willing to adjust and experiment to get the results you want. To preserve freshness, slice only what is being served. Store any leftover bread in an airtight container or wrapped in plastic wrap for up to three days (or three months in the freezer).

#2 Paleo breads often stick to the pan, so it is a prudent idea to grease your bakeware well and line with greased parchment whenever possible. Follow the directions, to the letter, about cooling as well because some loaves need to be completely cool before removing them from the pan. Otherwise they will crumble.

#3   Nut flours tend to be the base of most Paleo bread recipes, so it is important to be familiar with how they react during the baking process. Nut flours can burn easily, so keep your oven temperature low, no higher than 350 degrees F. To avoid burning, always watch your bread while it is baking, and if the top of your bread looks like it is browning too quickly, cover it with a piece of foil until the loaf is cooked through.

#4   If you want a finer-textured bread, take the time to grind your nuts very well. Don't go too far, though, or you will end up with nut butter instead of flour! If you buy a ground-nut product, pulse it in a food processor to grind the product more. The finer the ground nuts, the better your breads will turn out. Be aware that the consistency of your batter will be thicker than wheat-based recipes.

#5 Choose your oils carefully when baking Paleo breads. Avoid oils that are processed in a manner that makes them less healthy, such as canola oil and grapeseed oil. Coconut oil is a wonderful choice because it is sweet and imparts a great, yet usually subtle, flavor to baked products. Try to use unrefined, virgin, expeller- or cold-pressed coconut oil whenever possible. If you are creating your own recipes, coconut oil can be substituted 1:1 with other oils such as butter or shortening. Do not store your coconut oil in the refrigerator because it will become hard and difficult to blend.

#6 Paleo breads can sometimes incorporate dairy as long as it is grass fed and free of hormones as well as other additives. Products such as ghee and clarified butter can also be considered for Paleo baking because removing the milk solids takes out the sugars, proteins, and other elements that cause issues for those with dairy sensitivities. It is up to you to decide whether or not dairy is part of your Paleo experience.

#7   Remember that coconut flour does not behave like wheat flour. It is clumpy, dry, and unbelievably absorbent. You will need very little coconut flour in any recipe to produce a lovely result. You must make sure you beat this flour into your batter very well and let it sit for a few minutes to gauge the thickness of the batter. Since coconut flour is so dry, you will need to add lots of eggs, mashed bananas, or other liquids to offset this effect. However, if you use too much wet ingredients, your finished bread will be soggy and heavy. Baking with coconut flour may necessitate a steep learning curve; however, when you do master this ingredient, the results will be well worth the effort.

#8   Yeast can be used in Paleo baking even though it does not create exactly the same type of rise without the gluten. The active yeast used in baking is closely related to the beneficial yeast found in fermented foods, so they can be included without guilt or adverse health reactions. You must make sure you pay particularly close attention to temperature when proofing so you don't kill the yeast organisms.

#9 Coconut milk is a great substitute for dairy in your Paleo recipes. For convenience, use canned, full-fat, unsweetened coconut milk (often found in the Asian foods aisle at the grocery store). Unless otherwise specified in a recipe make sure you shake the coconut milk well before using it, because the water and fat will often separate in the can. If a recipe calls for coconut cream, simply open the can and scoop out the thick solid part that sits on top.

#10 Some of the products used to make Paleo bread, such as coconut and almond flours, are expensive. If you are going to make a lot of breads and baked products, try to get your ingredients in bulk to save money. Nut flours can be stored in the refrigerator or freezer with no ill effects as long as they are sealed well, so feel free to stock up.

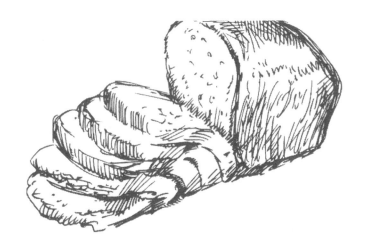

How can a nation be great if its bread tastes like Kleenex?

—Julia Child

2

SAVORY BREADS

Perfectly Perfect Sandwich Bread

Some Paleo enthusiasts are adamantly against using yeast in recipes. However, the active yeast used in baking is closely related to the beneficial yeast found in fermented foods, so it can be included without guilt or adverse health reactions. When making this lovely bread, take care because yeast can be a finicky ingredient that needs a very specific temperature to rise. If your water is below 100 degrees F, a leaking amino acid creates a sticky dough, and if the water heats to over 130 degrees F, the yeast will die. This bread is lovely for sandwiches or when toasted with a dab of almond butter.

- 1½ cups warm water (105–115 degrees F)
- 2 teaspoons active dry yeast
- 2 large eggs, lightly beaten
- ⅓ cup melted coconut oil, plus extra to grease loaf pan
- 4 teaspoons apple cider vinegar
- 4 teaspoons honey
- ¾ cup flaxseed meal
- 1⅓ cups tapioca flour
- 1¼ cups arrowroot powder
- 1 cup ground pumpkin seeds
- ⅔ cup sifted coconut flour
- 1 teaspoon sea salt

1. Pour the warm water into a large bowl and sprinkle the yeast on top. Let sit for about 5–10 minutes until the yeast starts to foam.

2. Add the eggs, coconut oil, apple cider vinegar, and honey to the yeast mixture, and stir to combine. Let mixture sit for about 3 minutes.

3. In a medium bowl, stir together the dry ingredients.

4. Add the dry ingredients to the wet ingredients and mix, by hand if you have to, until well incorporated.

5. Cover the bowl with a clean kitchen towel and place in a warm corner of the kitchen. Let rise for about 45 minutes to 1 hour.

6. Place the bread batter into a lightly greased, 9 x 5-inch loaf pan, and let it rise for another 45 minutes.

7. Preheat oven to 350 degrees F.

8. Bake the bread for 55–65 minutes, until the top is golden brown and a knife inserted in the center comes out clean.

9. Let the loaf cool for 10 minutes. Then turn it out onto a wire rack until ready to serve.

Makes 1 standard loaf (8–10 slices).

Jalapeño "Cornbread"

This recipe will remind you of golden cornbread served warm from the oven. Jalapeños provide subtle pleasing heat and contain capsaicin, which can help reduce the risk of certain types of cancer and cardiovascular disease. Make sure you wash your hands thoroughly after mincing your peppers because the juice can seriously irritate your eyes and mucous membranes.

- 4 large eggs, at room temperature
- 1 cup warm water
- 4 teaspoons apple cider vinegar
- ¼ teaspoon minced garlic
- ½ teaspoon minced jalapeño pepper
- ¼ cup melted coconut oil, plus extra to grease loaf pans
- ½ cup coconut flour
- ¼ teaspoon sea salt
- ½ tablespoon ground caraway seeds
- ½ teaspoon baking soda

1. Preheat oven to 350 degrees F and lightly grease two 2½ x 4½-inch mini loaf pans.

2. In a large bowl, beat together the eggs, water, apple cider vinegar, garlic, jalapeño pepper, and coconut oil until well combined.

3. In a small bowl, stir together the coconut flour, salt, caraway seeds, and baking soda.

4. Add the dry ingredients to the wet ingredients and stir until completely blended.

5. Spoon the batter into the two mini loaf pans, and bake for about 45 minutes, until a knife inserted in the center comes out clean.

6. Let the loaves cool for 10 minutes. Then turn them out onto a wire rack until ready to serve.

Makes 2 mini loaves (8–10 slices in total).

Spiced Zucchini Carrot Bread

The spicy scent of these cute mini loaves still warm from the oven will evoke memories of crisp fall days, cozy quilts, and time spent with family. The zucchini is not strongly apparent in the flavor, but it adds moistness to the bread, and both vegetables in this recipe are high in healthy beta-carotene. You can replace the zucchini with grated apple with wonderful results.

- 1½ cups sifted almond flour
- 1½ teaspoons baking soda
- ¼ teaspoon salt
- ½ teaspoon ground cinnamon
- ¼ teaspoon ground nutmeg
- ¼ teaspoon ground ginger
- 3 large eggs
- 3 tablespoons pure maple syrup
- 1 tablespoon melted coconut oil, plus extra to grease loaf pans
- 1 cup grated zucchini, squeezed out
- 1 cup finely grated carrot
- Almond flour to dust loaf pans

1. Preheat oven to 350 degrees F.

2. In a small bowl, stir together the dry ingredients.

3. In a large bowl, whisk together the eggs, maple syrup, and coconut oil for about 3 minutes.

4. Whisk the zucchini and carrot into the wet ingredients until well blended.

5. Add the dry ingredients to the wet ingredients and stir until combined.

6. Lightly grease two 2½ x 4½-inch mini loaf pans and dust with the almond flour.

7. Spoon the batter evenly into the loaf pans, and bake the bread for 35 minutes, until a knife inserted in the center comes out clean.

8. Let the loaves cool for 10 minutes. Then turn them out onto a wire rack until ready to serve.

Makes 2 mini loaves (8–10 slices in total).

Amazing Multigrain Bread

*Sometimes nothing will do but a nutty, crunchy, and seedy bread to top
with slices of shaved beef or a perfectly grilled chicken breast. This bread
has enough substance to hold up to any sandwich filling, and the perfect
taste to be enjoyed with a little almond butter or even plain. You can easily
add more seeds or adjust the types used to create exactly the right flavor.*

- 1½ cups almond flour
- ¾ cup arrowroot powder
- ¼ cup flaxseed meal
- ¼ teaspoon sea salt
- ½ teaspoon baking soda
- 4 large eggs
- 2 teaspoons honey
- 1 teaspoon apple cider vinegar
- 2 tablespoons sesame seeds
- ½ cup hulled raw sunflower seeds
- Coconut oil to grease the loaf pan

1. Preheat oven to 350 degrees F and lightly grease a 9 x 5-inch loaf pan.

2. In a medium bowl, stir together the almond flour, arrowroot powder, flaxseed meal, salt, and baking soda.

3. In a large bowl, beat the eggs with a hand mixer or a whisk until very thick and frothy, about 5 minutes.

4. Beat the honey and apple cider vinegar into the eggs.

5. Gently fold the dry ingredients into the egg mixture until thoroughly mixed.

6. Fold in sesame seeds and sunflower seeds.

7. Spoon the batter into the loaf pan, and bake for 40–45 minutes, until a knife inserted in the center comes out clean.

8. Let the loaf cool for 10 minutes before turning it out onto a wire rack. Serve warm whenever possible.

Makes 1 standard loaf (8–10 slices).

Easy Paleo Bread

This recipe is a very basic Paleo approach to bread making. Most Paleo breads have vinegar, a sweetener, eggs, coconut oil, and various flours combined to form the loaf. If you are feeling creative, you can use this recipe as a base to experiment with spices, dried fruit, seeds, and even chocolate. The only real rule is to make sure the loaf pan is not too big or the finished bread will not be the proper height.

• 2 cups almond flour	• 2 teaspoons melted coconut oil, plus extra to grease loaf pan
• 4 teaspoons coconut flour	
• ⅓ cup flaxseed meal	• 1 tablespoon honey
• ½ teaspoon baking soda	• 1 tablespoon apple cider vinegar
• ¼ teaspoon sea salt	
• 5 large eggs	

1. Preheat oven to 350 degrees F and lightly grease a 7½ x 3½-inch loaf pan.

2. In a large bowl, stir together the almond flour, coconut flour, flaxseed meal, baking soda, and salt.

3. In a small bowl, whisk together the eggs, coconut oil, honey, and apple cider vinegar until well combined.

4. Add the egg mixture to the dry ingredients and stir to mix evenly.

5. Spoon the batter into the loaf pan, and bake for 30–35 minutes, until a knife inserted in the center comes out clean.

6. Let the loaf cool for 10 minutes. Then turn it out onto a wire rack until ready to serve.

Makes 1 medium loaf (6–8 slices).

Paleo "Egg" Bread

The tender texture of most traditional egg breads is what makes it so wonderful when warm and slathered with jam. You can omit the sesame seeds, but they do add a nice nutty taste and a delicate little crunch. This loaf can brown quickly, so check it about halfway through the bake time and place a sheet of foil over the loaf to get exactly the right color.

- 2½ cups ground almond meal
- ⅓ cup tapioca flour
- ¾ teaspoon baking soda
- ¼ teaspoon sea salt
- 7 large eggs, at room temperature, separated
- ⅓ cup melted coconut oil, plus extra to grease loaf pan
- ⅓ cup coconut milk
- 4 teaspoons pure maple syrup
- 1 tablespoon sesame seeds

1. Preheat oven to 325 degrees F.

2. In a large bowl, stir together the almond meal, tapioca flour, baking soda, and salt until well combined.

3. In a small bowl, whisk together the egg yolks (reserving the whites), coconut oil, coconut milk, and maple syrup.

4. Stir the egg yolk mixture into the dry ingredients until smooth.

5. In a medium bowl, whisk the egg whites until they form moist, firm peaks.

6. Stir about one-third of the beaten egg whites into the batter to lighten it.

7. Carefully fold the remaining whites into the batter, taking care not to overmix.

8. Lightly grease a 9 x 5-inch loaf pan and line the bottom with parchment paper. Lightly oil the parchment.

9. Spoon the batter into the prepared pan, smoothing the top and sprinkling with sesame seeds.

10. Bake for 40–45 minutes, until a knife inserted in the center comes out clean.

11. Let the loaf cool for 10 minutes. Then turn it out onto a wire rack until ready to serve.

Makes 1 standard loaf (7–9 slices).

Paleo Almond Bread

Almond flour is a staple ingredient in Paleo bread, and this recipe takes it a step further by incorporating creamy almond butter and sliced almonds, as well. Almonds can help lower cholesterol, reduce the risk of heart attack, and help build healthy bones and teeth. If you want richer-tasting bread, replace the almond components with exact quantities of cashew ingredients.

- ¾ cup almond butter
- 6 large eggs
- 4 teaspoons pure maple syrup
- ¼ cup melted coconut oil, plus extra to grease loaf pan
- ¼ cup flaxseed meal
- ¼ cup almond flour
- 4 teaspoons coconut flour
- ½ teaspoon baking soda
- ½ teaspoon salt
- 2 tablespoons toasted sliced almonds

1. Preheat oven to 350 degrees F and generously grease an 8 x 4-inch loaf pan.

2. In a large bowl, blend together the almond butter, eggs, maple syrup, and coconut oil with a hand mixer or whisk until smooth.

3. In a small bowl, combine the flaxseed meal, almond four, coconut flour, baking soda, and salt.

4. Add the dry ingredients to the wet ingredients and blend together.

5. Spoon the batter into the loaf pan, sprinkle the almonds on top, and bake for 35–40 minutes, until a knife inserted in the center comes out clean.

6. Allow the bread to cool for 15 minutes, and then run a knife around the edges to remove from the pan.

7. Serve warm or cold.

Makes 1 small loaf (6–8 slices).

Chia Paleo Bread

Chia seeds are smaller than sesame seeds and have a very mild flavor, which combines well with other ingredients. They are a wonderful source of omega-3 fatty acids and fiber and have been linked to lowering cholesterol, stabilizing blood sugar, and boosting energy. This recipe makes a small loaf, but it will pack a powerful nutritional punch, especially if you have a couple slices for breakfast.

- 1½ cups almond flour
- ½ cup coconut flour
- ¼ cup ground chia seeds
- ½ teaspoon baking soda
- ¼ teaspoon sea salt
- 5 large eggs
- 4 tablespoons melted coconut oil, plus extra to grease loaf pan
- 1 tablespoon apple cider vinegar

1. Preheat oven to 350 degrees F and lightly grease an 8 x 4-inch loaf pan.

2. In a large bowl, stir together the almond flour, coconut flour, chia seeds, baking soda, and salt until well combined.

3. In a small bowl, whisk together the eggs, coconut oil, and apple cider vinegar.

4. Add the wet ingredients to the dry ingredients and stir until incorporated completely.

5. Spoon into loaf pan and smooth the top.

6. Bake for 40–50 minutes, until a knife inserted in the center comes out clean.

7. Let the loaf cool for 10 minutes. Then turn it out onto a wire rack until completely cool.

Makes 1 small loaf (4–6 slices).

Basic Paleo Bread

Bread can have charm when it is unapologetically plain but satisfying. This recipe produces a good, simple-to-prepare loaf that can be used with any filling or topping because there is no extra spicing or flavors to interfere. The finished loaf here is quite small, so if you need a bigger sandwich, cut the loaf lengthwise to create long pieces.

- 4 large eggs
- ¼ cup melted coconut oil, plus extra to grease loaf pan
- 1 teaspoon apple cider vinegar
- ¼ cup coconut flour
- ¼ cup tapioca flour
- ½ teaspoon cream of tartar
- ¼ teaspoon baking soda

1. Preheat oven to 350 degrees F.

2. In a medium bowl, whisk the eggs until frothy.

3. Add the melted coconut oil and apple cider vinegar to the eggs and whisk until blended.

4. Add the remaining ingredients and beat until smooth. Let the batter sit for about 5 minutes.

5. Grease an 8 x 4-inch loaf pan lightly with coconut oil. Line the pan with parchment paper and lightly oil the paper.

6. Spoon the batter into the prepared pan and smooth the top.

7. Bake for 30–35 minutes, until a knife inserted in the center comes out clean.

8. Let the loaf cool for 10 minutes. Then turn it out onto a wire rack until ready to serve.

Makes 1 small loaf (4–6 slices).

Quinoa Sandwich Bread

Quinoa is one of those ingredients that seem to be in dispute for many people following a Paleo lifestyle. Many people do not know that quinoa is actually a seed, which places it well within Paleo territory. However, it does create some of the same issues as grains, which makes it an uncertain choice. Basically, if you have no adverse reactions when eating quinoa, try this wonderful, nutty-tasting bread for your sandwiches and morning toast.

- 1 cup whole white quinoa
- 2 large eggs
- ¼ cup coconut flour
- 1 tablespoon melted coconut oil plus extra to grease pan
- 1 tablespoon water
- 1 tablespoon raw honey

---

1. Preheat oven to 350 degrees F and lightly grease a 9 x 5-inch loaf pan.

2. Place the quinoa in a powerful blender, food processor, or clean coffee grinder, and process until it becomes a fine flour. Alternately, substitute pre-ground quinoa flour.

3. In a medium bowl, using an electric mixer, beat the eggs until light yellow and frothy.

4. In a large bowl, stir together the quinoa, coconut flour, and coconut oil until well combined. Stir in the water.

5. Add the eggs and honey to the flour mixture and stir until well combined.

6. Allow the dough to rest for 5 minutes, then stir again, adding a little more water if necessary to make the dough pliable and easy to knead.

7. The dough should be lightly sticky, but not wet. Allow the dough to rest for 5 more minutes.

8. Place the dough in the loaf pan, and bake for 30–35 minutes, until the top of the bread is golden brown.

9. Let the loaf cool for 10 minutes. Then turn it out onto a wire rack until ready to serve.

Makes 1 standard loaf (8–10 slices).

Herbed Flax Bread

The tantalizing scent of baking herbs will draw everyone in the house to the kitchen to wait for a slice of this savory treat. This bread is best made with fresh herbs, but dried can be used as well—just adjust the quantities to 1 teaspoon dried instead of 1 tablespoon fresh. You can also substitute other favorite herbs such as marjoram or basil to create your own special blend.

- 1½ cups almond flour
- 3 tablespoons flaxseed meal
- 2 tablespoons coconut flour
- 1 tablespoon chopped fresh rosemary
- 1 teaspoon chopped fresh thyme
- 1 teaspoon chopped fresh oregano
- 1½ teaspoons baking soda
- ¼ teaspoon sea salt
- 5 large eggs
- ¼ cup melted coconut oil plus extra to grease loaf pan
- 1 tablespoon apple cider vinegar

1. Preheat oven to 350 degrees F and lightly grease a 9 x 5-inch loaf pan.

2. In a large bowl, stir together the almond flour, flaxseed meal, coconut flour, herbs, baking soda, and salt until very well mixed.

3. In a small bowl, whisk together the eggs, coconut oil, and apple cider vinegar.

4. Add the wet ingredients to the dry ingredients and stir to combine.

5. Spoon batter into the loaf pan and bake for 30–35 minutes, until a knife inserted in the center comes out clean.

6. Let the loaf cool for 10 minutes. Then turn it out onto a wire rack until ready to serve.

Makes 1 standard loaf (8–10 slices).

Kalamata Olive Bread

This bistro-style bread is wonderful for thick Italian meat sandwiches slathered with roasted red pepper spread or topped with ripe tomato slices. The recipe calls for kalamata olives, but any kind will do if you have them on hand. If you are using a saltier green olive, you might want to reduce the salt used in the dough to offset the green olives. This recipe can also be pressed flat on a baking sheet for focaccia-style bread.

- ¼ cup almond flour
- ¼ cup arrowroot powder
- 1 teaspoon baking soda
- 3 large eggs
- ¾ cup raw cashew butter
- ½ cup pitted and chopped kalamata olives
- 1 tablespoon extra-virgin olive oil, plus extra to grease loaf pan

1. Preheat oven to 350 degrees F and lightly grease a 9 x 5-inch loaf pan.

2. In a medium bowl, stir together the almond flour, arrowroot powder, and baking soda until well combined.

3. In a large bowl, using an electric mixer, beat the eggs and cashew butter until well combined.

4. Add the flour mixture to the wet ingredients and stir until a wet dough forms.

5. Fold in the olives.

6. Spread the batter into the loaf pan, and drizzle the olive oil over the top.

7. Bake for 25–30 minutes, until the top of the bread is golden brown.

8. Let the loaf cool for 10 minutes. Then turn it out onto a wire rack until completely cool.

Makes 1 standard loaf (8–10 slices).

Country-Style White Bread

This can be your all-round, go-to bread for sandwiches, toast, and even breadcrumbs because it has such a simple wholesome taste. A plain white bread is sometimes exactly what is needed, and this country-style loaf will be perfect. This recipe does not make a large, high loaf, so if you need a bit more height, try reducing the size of the loaf pan a little and adjust the bake time to about 5 to 10 minutes longer, watching carefully.

- 1 cup almond flour
- ½ cup arrowroot powder
- 1 teaspoon baking soda
- 1 teaspoon cream of tartar
- 3 large eggs
- 2 tablespoons melted coconut oil, plus extra to grease pan
- 2 tablespoons water
- 1 teaspoon honey

1. Preheat oven to 350 degrees F and lightly grease a 9 x 5-inch loaf pan.

2. In a medium bowl, stir together the almond flour, arrowroot powder, baking soda, and cream of tartar until well combined.

3. In a large bowl, using an electric mixer, beat the eggs until frothy. Add the coconut oil, water, and honey, and stir to combine.

4. Add the flour mixture to the wet ingredients and stir until just combined.

5. Pour the batter into the loaf pan, and bake for 25–30 minutes, until the top of the bread is golden brown.

6. Let the loaf cool for 10 minutes. Then turn it out onto a wire rack until completely cool.

Makes 1 standard loaf (8–10 slices).

Rosemary and Thyme Bread

This is quite a light bread for one that does not contain yeast or wheat flour and is baked flat. It can also be adjusted to reflect whatever you are serving with it. Feel free to change the herbs to your favorites or to whatever is fresh in your garden, including a lovely lemon balm or even peppermint.

- ¼ cup almond flour
- ¼ cup arrowroot powder
- 1 teaspoon baking soda
- ¾ cup raw almond butter
- 1 tablespoon raw honey
- 3 large eggs
- 2 tablespoons finely chopped fresh thyme
- 1 tablespoon finely chopped fresh oregano
- 1 tablespoon finely chopped fresh rosemary
- Olive oil to grease jelly-roll pan

1. Preheat oven to 350 degrees F.

2. In a small bowl, stir together the almond flour, arrowroot powder, and baking soda until combined.

3. In a large bowl, using an electric mixer, beat the almond butter and honey. Then add the eggs, one at a time, mixing after each addition. Add the herbs, and stir until combined.

4. Add the flour mixture to the wet ingredients and stir until a wet dough forms.

5. Line a 9 x 13-inch jelly-roll pan with parchment paper. Drizzle olive oil on the parchment-lined pan and spread the dough over it.

6. Bake for 25–30 minutes, until the top of the bread is golden brown.

7. Let the loaf cool for 10 minutes. Then turn it out onto a wire rack until ready to serve.

Makes 1 large flatbread (12 squares).

Honey-Scented Sandwich Bread

When you try this lovely bread, you might think it actually contains wheat because the flaxseeds have a similar bulk and texture. Flaxseed is a great source of heart-friendly fats and fiber. This bread is perfect for hearty sandwiches and when toasted with a bit of Paleo-approved jam.

- 1 cup almond flour
- ½ cup flaxseed meal
- 1 teaspoon baking soda
- 1 teaspoon cream of tartar
- 3 large eggs

- 2 tablespoons melted coconut oil plus extra to grease loaf pan
- 2 tablespoons water
- 2 tablespoons raw honey

1. Preheat oven to 350 degrees F and lightly grease a 9 x 5-inch loaf pan.

2. In a medium bowl, stir together the almond flour, flaxseed meal, baking soda, and cream of tartar until well combined.

3. In a large bowl, using an electric mixer, beat the eggs until frothy. Add the coconut oil, water, and honey, and stir until well combined.

4. Add the flour mixture to the wet ingredients and stir until well combined.

5. Pour the batter into the loaf pan, and bake for 25–30 minutes, until the top of the bread is dark brown.

6. Allow the bread to cool completely on a wire rack before removing it from the pan.

Makes 1 standard loaf (8–10 slices).

Winter Squash Bread

Winter squash is not as strange an ingredient as you might think for a quick bread. It tastes a great deal like pumpkin and can be combined with the same types of spices and sweeteners with great success. Sunflower seeds provide a nice crunch, while the hint of honey provides a perfect backdrop for any sandwich topping.

- 3 cups finely grated raw winter squash
- 4 large eggs
- ¼ cup melted coconut oil, plus extra to grease loaf pan
- 2 tablespoons honey
- 1 tablespoon fresh lemon juice
- 3 cups almond flour
- ¾ teaspoon baking soda
- ½ teaspoon sea salt
- ½ teaspoon ground nutmeg
- 2 tablespoons hulled raw sunflower seeds

1. Preheat oven to 325 degrees F.

2. In a large bowl, stir together the squash, eggs, ¼ cup of coconut oil, honey, and lemon juice until well mixed.

3. In a medium bowl, stir together the almond flour, baking soda, salt, and nutmeg.

4. Add the dry ingredients to the wet ingredients and stir until well incorporated.

5. Lightly grease a 9 x 5-inch loaf pan, and line the bottom with parchment paper. Grease the paper.

6. Spoon the batter into the pan, and sprinkle the top with the sunflower seeds.

7. Bake for about 1–1½ hours, until a knife inserted in the center comes out clean.

8. Allow bread to cool in the loaf pan for at least 1 hour before removing it from the pan.

Makes 1 standard loaf (8–10 slices).

Skinny Flax Bread

Egg whites are used here instead of all whole eggs, which reduces calories in the finished product. Because most people start a Paleo lifestyle to become healthier, this might be an important consideration. The egg whites add a certain lightness to the batter without the effort of having to whip them up. You can easily substitute nutmeg instead of cinnamon for the spices, and try the recipe with maple syrup instead of honey if you'd like.

- 2 cups flaxseed meal
- 1 tablespoon baking powder
- 1 teaspoon sea salt
- ½ teaspoon cinnamon
- 5 large egg whites
- 2 large eggs
- ¼ cup melted coconut oil, plus extra to grease loaf pan
- ½ cup honey
- ¼ cup water

1. Preheat oven to 350 degrees F and lightly grease an 8 x 4-inch loaf pan

2. In a large bowl, stir together the flaxseed meal, baking powder, salt, and cinnamon.

3. In a medium bowl, whisk together the egg whites, eggs, ¼ cup of coconut oil, honey, and water.

4. Mix the wet ingredients into the dry ingredients and stir to combine.

5. Spoon the batter into the loaf pan and smooth the top.

6. Bake for 15–20 minutes, until a knife inserted in the center comes out clean.

7. Let the loaf cool for 10 minutes. Then turn it out onto a wire rack until ready to serve.

Makes 1 small loaf (6–8 slices).

Chock-Full-of-Nuts Bread

Nuts, seeds, a touch of honey, . . . and more nuts! The finished loaf is not overly large, but each slice is packed with heart-healthy nutrients, protein, and fiber, so you won't need huge portions to be satisfied. You can adjust the measurements of nuts and seeds in the recipe as long as the finished amount is the same. Experiment to see what combination works best for your palate.

- 1½ cups almond flour
- ½ cup arrowroot powder
- 1½ teaspoons baking powder
- ½ teaspoon sea salt
- 4 large eggs
- 4 tablespoons water
- 2 teaspoons honey
- 3 tablespoons melted coconut oil, plus extra to grease loaf pan
- ¼ cup hulled raw sunflower seeds
- ¼ cup sesame seeds
- ¼ cup chopped pecans
- ¼ cup chopped pistachios
- ¼ cup pumpkin seeds

1. Preheat oven to 350 degrees F and lightly grease a 7½ x 3½-inch loaf pan.

2. In a large bowl, combine the almond flour, arrowroot powder, baking powder, and salt until well mixed.

3. In a small bowl, whisk together the eggs, water, honey, and 3 tablespoons of coconut oil.

4. Add the wet ingredients to the dry ingredients and stir to incorporate. Stir in the seeds and chopped nuts.

5. Spoon the batter into the loaf pan and smooth out the top.

6. Bake for 40–45 minutes, until a knife inserted in the center comes out clean.

7. Let the loaf cool for 10 minutes. Then turn it out onto a wire rack until ready to serve.

Makes 1 medium loaf (6–8 slices).

Tender Paleo Bread

Paleo bread is sometimes thought to be dense, but this recipe creates a lovely, textured bread that's perfect for dipping in soup and sopping up juices from a nice roast. The egg whites and arrowroot powder are what make this bread so tender, so don't substitute other ingredients for these in the recipe.

- 1½ cups arrowroot powder
- 1 cup flaxseed meal
- 2 tablespoons baking powder
- 1 tablespoon sea salt

- 4 large eggs
- 4 large egg whites
- ¼ cup melted coconut oil, plus extra to grease loaf pan
- 1 tablespoon apple cider vinegar

1. Preheat oven to 350 degrees F and lightly grease a 9 x 5-inch loaf pan.

2. In a large bowl, stir together the arrowroot powder, flaxseed meal, baking powder, and salt.

3. In a medium bowl whisk together the eggs, egg whites, coconut oil, and apple cider vinegar until well combined.

4. Add the wet ingredients to the dry ingredients and stir to mix well.

5. Spoon the batter into the loaf pan and smooth the top.

6. Bake for 35–40 minutes, until a knife inserted in the center comes out clean.

7. Let the loaf cool for 10 minutes. Then turn it out onto a wire rack until ready to serve.

Makes 1 standard loaf (8–10 slices).

"Rye" Bread

This loaf is quite small, but the flavor is a wonderful accompaniment to sliced meat sandwiches and healthy dips. You can get four healthy-sized portions if you slice this loaf lengthwise through the middle instead of the usual way. The caraway seeds are very important for creating a "rye" taste in this loaf, so do not omit them. They are also a rich source of dietary fiber, calcium, iron, copper, and potassium.

- 1 cup almond flour
- ¾ cup flaxseed meal
- ¾ teaspoon cream of tartar
- ½ teaspoon baking soda
- ½ teaspoon sea salt
- 3 large eggs
- ¼ cup water
- 2 tablespoons melted coconut oil, plus extra to grease loaf pan
- 1 teaspoon honey
- 4 teaspoons caraway seeds, divided

1. Preheat oven to 350 degrees F and lightly grease an 8 x 4-inch loaf pan.

2. In a large bowl, stir together the almond flour, flaxseed meal, cream of tartar, baking soda, and salt.

3. In a small bowl, whisk the eggs, water, 2 tablespoons of coconut oil, and honey until well blended.

4. Add the wet ingredients to the dry ingredients and stir to combine. Stir in 3 teaspoons of caraway seeds.

5. Spoon the batter into the loaf pan, sprinkle with the remaining caraway seeds, and let it sit 5 minutes before putting the pan into the oven.

6. Bake for about 35 minutes, until a knife inserted into the center comes out clean.

7. Let the loaf cool for 10 minutes. Then turn it out onto a wire rack until completely cool.

Makes 1 small loaf (6–8 small slices).

Simple Coconut Bread

Sweet vanilla, shredded coconut, and honey create a fragrant, easy-to-prepare loaf that will suit all your Paleo needs in one delicious package. If you can use fresh coconut rather than a preshredded product, you will find your bread has a more complex and richer taste.

- 6 large eggs
- 2 teaspoons pure vanilla extract
- 2 tablespoons raw honey
- 3 cups unsweetened shredded coconut
- 1 teaspoon baking powder
- Coconut oil to grease loaf pan

1. Preheat oven to 300 degrees F and lightly grease a 9 x 5-inch loaf pan.

2. In a large bowl, using an electric mixer, beat the eggs, vanilla, and honey until frothy and well combined.

3. Place the shredded coconut in a food processor and pulse until it becomes a fine flour, being careful not to overprocess it. Add the baking powder to the coconut flour, and stir gently to combine.

4. Add the flour mixture to the wet ingredients and stir until just combined.

5. Pour the batter into the loaf pan.

6. Bake for 35–40 minutes, until a knife inserted into the center comes out clean.

7. Allow the bread to cool completely on a wire rack before removing it from the pan.

Makes 1 standard loaf (8–10 slices).

Five-Ingredient Paleo Bread

Paleo bread has never been so easy. If you need a plain, good-tasting, all-purpose bread, this is the best recipe to try. Egg protein is easily found in most mainstream grocery stores and bodybuilding shops. After mastering the recipe, you can get more creative with spices, nuts, and different types of egg-white protein flavors such as chocolate and vanilla custard.

- 1½ cups liquid egg whites
- 1 cup egg-white protein
- 1 cup unsweetened applesauce
- 9 tablespoons coconut flour
- 1 teaspoon baking soda
- Coconut oil to grease loaf pan

1. Preheat oven to 350 degrees F and lightly grease a 9 x 5-inch loaf pan.

2. Place all the ingredients in a large bowl and beat with a hand mixer or whisk for at least 5–7 minutes or until very fluffy.

3. Spoon the batter into the loaf pan, and bake for about 45 minutes, until a knife inserted in the center comes out clean.

4. Let the loaf cool for 10 minutes. Then turn it out onto a wire rack until ready to serve.

Makes 1 standard loaf (8–10 slices).

Hint-of-Heat Avocado Bread

Avocado is a wonderful Paleo bread ingredient, and the finished bread is rich-tasting but quite dense. Avocado is a super food, which should be included in your diet whenever possible. This fruit is packed full of protein, lutein, oleic acid, and folate. This means they are good for the heart and eyes and are great for pregnant women. Even though avocado is high in fat, it will make you feel full, which is important for weight management. Make sure your avocados are ripe and soft for this recipe, or the texture of the loaf will not be perfect.

- ½ cup flaxseed meal
- 1 teaspoon baking soda
- 1 teaspoon salt
- Pinch of cayenne, or to taste
- 6 large eggs
- 1 cup very smoothly pureed avocado (about 2 large ripe avocados)
- Coconut oil to grease loaf pan

1. Preheat oven to 350 degrees F and lightly grease a 9 x 5-inch loaf pan.

2. In a large bowl, stir together the flaxseed meal, baking soda, salt, and cayenne until well mixed.

3. In a medium bowl, whisk the eggs and avocado together.

4. Add the wet ingredients to the dry ingredients and stir together until it is a smooth batter.

5. Spoon the batter into the loaf pan and smooth the top.

6. Bake for about 50 minutes, until a knife inserted in the center comes out clean.

7. Let the loaf cool for 10 minutes. Then turn it out onto a wire rack until ready to serve.

Makes 1 standard loaf (8–10 slices).

Apple Tahini Bread

Anyone who enjoys African, Middle Eastern, and Greek food will be familiar with tahini, a paste created from ground hulled sesame seeds. This ingredient has a superb, unique toasty flavor and looks a little like natural peanut butter. It often has an oily film on top, which needs to be stirred into the paste before measuring it out for the recipe. You can find tahini in most grocery stores or in specialty gourmet food shops.

- ½ cup coconut flour
- ½ cup flaxseed meal
- 2 teaspoons cinnamon
- 1 teaspoon sea salt
- 1 teaspoon baking soda
- 6 large eggs, lightly beaten
- ½ cup unsweetened applesauce
- ½ large apple, peeled and diced
- ½ cup tahini
- ¼ cup pure maple syrup
- 2 teaspoons pure vanilla extract
- Coconut oil to grease loaf pan

1. Preheat oven to 350 degrees F and lightly grease a 9 x 5-inch loaf pan.

2. In a large bowl, stir together the coconut flour, flaxseed meal, cinnamon, salt, and baking soda until combined.

3. Make a well in the center of the dry ingredients and add the eggs, applesauce, apple, tahini, maple syrup, and vanilla. Stir until the batter is well blended.

4. Pour the batter into the loaf pan.

5. Bake for 45 minutes, until a knife inserted in the center comes out clean.

6. Let the loaf cool for 10 minutes. Then turn it out onto a wire rack until ready to serve.

Makes 1 standard loaf (8–10 slices).

Sunflower Bread

Sunflower seeds are commonly used in non-Paleo breads because they provide density, crunch, and an assortment of health benefits. These popular seeds are full of fiber, heart-healthful fats, and even a little protein. If you want even more texture and a richer taste, dry roast the seeds before mixing them into the batter.

- 1 cup almond flour
- ½ cup flaxseed meal
- 1 teaspoon baking soda
- 1 teaspoon cream of tartar
- 3 large eggs
- 2 tablespoons extra-virgin olive oil
- 2 tablespoons water
- 1 teaspoon honey
- ½ cup hulled raw sunflower seeds, divided
- Coconut oil to grease loaf pan

1. Preheat oven to 350 degrees F and lightly grease a 9 x 5-inch loaf pan.

2. In a medium bowl, stir together the almond flour, flaxseed meal, baking soda, and cream of tartar until well combined.

3. In a large bowl, using an electric mixer, beat the eggs until frothy, and then stir in the olive oil, water, and honey.

4. Add the flour mixture to the wet ingredients and stir until just combined. Fold in ¼ cup of the sunflower seeds.

5. Pour the batter into the loaf pan, sprinkle with the remaining sunflower seeds, and bake for 25–30 minutes, until the top of the bread is dark brown.

6. Allow the bread to cool completely on a wire rack before removing it from the pan.

Makes 1 standard loaf (8–10 slices).

Sesame Honey Bread

There is something magical about the scent and flavor of toasted sesame seeds. A few of these nutritious seeds goes a long way, so don't be tempted to throw in more than what the recipe calls for. This loaf is not very high, but it can still be used for sandwiches.

- 3½ cups almond flour
- 3 tablespoons sesame seeds, divided
- 1 teaspoon sea salt
- 1 teaspoon baking soda
- ¼ teaspoon baking powder
- 4 large eggs, separated
- 1 tablespoon honey
- 1 teaspoon apple cider vinegar
- Coconut oil to grease loaf pan

1. Preheat oven to 350 degrees F.

2. In a medium bowl, stir together the almond flour, 2 tablespoons of the sesame seeds, sea salt, baking soda, and baking powder.

3. In a large bowl, whisk together the egg yolks, honey, and apple cider vinegar until blended.

4. Add the dry ingredients to the yolk mixture and stir to combine.

5. In a medium bowl, whisk or beat the egg whites until they are about double in volume.

6. Fold the egg whites into the batter gently until incorporated.

7. Spoon the bread batter into a lightly greased, 9 x 5-inch loaf pan, and sprinkle the top with the remaining sesame seeds.

8. Bake for about 20 minutes, until a knife inserted in the center comes out clean.

9. Let the loaf cool for 10 minutes. Then turn it out onto a wire rack until ready to serve.

Makes 1 standard loaf (8–10 slices).

Honey Yeast Bread

Yeast can be intimidating for some bakers, but this recipe is very simple. The trick is to find the perfect spot, not too warm or cool, to let the bread rise. Also, don't omit the honey because yeast needs sugar to break down to carbon dioxide and alcohol, which makes the bread rise. This bread might become your new family favorite sandwich bread.

- 1 cup warm water (105–115 degrees F)
- 2 teaspoons active dry yeast
- 2 large eggs
- ¼ cup melted coconut oil, plus extra to grease loaf pan
- 2 tablespoons honey
- 1 tablespoon apple cider vinegar
- 4 cups almond flour
- ⅔ cup tapioca flour
- ⅔ cup arrowroot powder
- ½ cup flaxseed meal

1. Pour the warm water into a large bowl, and sprinkle the yeast on top. Let sit for about 5–10 minutes until the yeast starts to foam.

2. Add the eggs, coconut oil, honey, and apple cider vinegar to the yeast mixture and stir to combine.

3. In a small bowl, stir together the almond flour, tapioca flour, arrowroot powder, and flaxseed meal until well combined.

4. Add the dry ingredients to the yeast mixture and stir to combine well.

5. Place a clean cloth over the bowl and place the bowl in a warm area in the kitchen to let the batter rise for about 1 hour.

6. Spoon the batter into a lightly greased 9 x 5-inch loaf pan and smooth the top. Let batter rise again for about 1 hour.

7. Preheat oven to 375 degrees F.

8. Bake for 45–50 minutes, until golden on top and a knife inserted in the center comes out clean.

9. Let the loaf cool for 10 minutes. Then turn it out onto a wire rack until ready to serve.

Makes 1 standard loaf (8–10 slices).

Traditional Irish Soda Bread

Soda bread is a good choice for no-yeast Paleo dieters because it uses baking soda instead of yeast. These loaves are not baked in loaf pans, but rather free-form on baking sheets, so make sure you don't flatten the dough out too much or your bread will be equally flat. You can substitute raisins for the currants if that is your preference, although the currants add a nice tart flavor to the finished loaf.

- 2¾ cups almond flour
- ½ cup of tapioca flour, plus extra for dusting
- 1½ teaspoons baking soda
- ½ teaspoon baking powder
- Dash of sea salt
- ½ cup dried currants
- ½ teaspoon caraway seeds
- 3 large eggs
- 1 tablespoon apple cider vinegar
- 1 tablespoon honey

1. Preheat oven to 350 degrees F.

2. In a large bowl, stir together the almond flour, tapioca flour, baking soda, baking powder, salt, currants, and caraway seeds until well mixed.

3. In a small bowl, whisk together the eggs, apple cider vinegar, and honey until combined.

4. Add the wet ingredients to the dry ingredients and mix until the dough holds together.

5. Put a sheet of parchment paper on a small cookie sheet. Place the dough onto the cookie sheet and dust the top with a little tapioca flour. Use your hands to form the dough into a round loaf about 2 inches high and 6–7 inches across.

6. Score an X in the top of the loaf with a knife to create the traditional soda-bread style.

7. Bake for 35–40 minutes until lightly golden.

8. Let the loaf cool for 10 minutes. Then turn it out onto a wire rack until ready to serve.

Makes 1 loaf (6–8 slices).

Savory Rosemary Bread

Rosemary is a pungent Mediterranean herb used in many culinary applications, including the flavoring in delicious bread. Rosemary also has many health benefits, including cancer prevention, mood enhancement, and immune system improvement. Use fresh rosemary in this recipe to get the best health benefits, and make sure you chop the herb very finely because big pieces are unpalatable.

- ½ cup coconut flour
- ⅓ cup flaxseed meal
- 1 teaspoon baking soda
- 1 teaspoon sea salt
- 4 large eggs
- ¼ cup melted coconut oil, plus extra to grease loaf pan
- ¼ cup coconut milk
- 2 teaspoons chopped fresh rosemary

1. Preheat oven to 350 degrees F and lightly grease an 8 x 4-inch loaf pan.

2. In a small bowl, combine the coconut flour, flaxseed meal, baking soda, and salt.

3. In a large bowl, beat together the eggs, coconut oil, coconut milk, and rosemary until well mixed.

4. Add the dry ingredients to the wet ingredients and stir until smooth.

5. Spoon the batter into the loaf pan.

6. Bake bread for 35–45 minutes, until a knife inserted in the center comes out clean.

7. Let the loaf cool for 10 minutes. Then turn it out onto a wire rack until completely cool.

Makes 1 small loaf (6–8 slices).

All sorrows are less with bread.

—Miguel de Cervantes

3

SWEET BREADS

Tropical Banana Bread

Great banana bread is a valuable staple recipe because it can be a perfect gift, a satisfying snack, and an energy-packed way to start the day. Bananas contain potassium, which can help regulate blood pressure and help muscles to contract properly without cramping up. The warm spices in this recipe also have health benefits such as regulating healthy glucose levels in the blood and lowering blood pressure.

- ¾ cup almond flour
- ¼ cup coconut flour
- ¾ teaspoon baking soda
- ¾ teaspoon baking powder
- ½ teaspoon sea salt
- ¾ teaspoon ground cinnamon
- ¼ teaspoon ground ginger
- ¼ teaspoon ground nutmeg
- 2 large eggs
- ⅓ cup pure maple syrup
- 2 tablespoons melted coconut oil, plus extra to grease loaf pan
- 1 teaspoon pure vanilla extract
- 2 large, very ripe bananas, mashed
- ¼ cup shredded unsweetened coconut
- Almond flour to dust loaf pan

1. Preheat oven to 350 degrees F.

2. In a large bowl, sift together the flours, baking soda, baking powder, salt, and spices.

3. In a small bowl, whisk together the eggs, maple syrup, coconut oil, and vanilla until well combined. Whisk the banana and shredded coconut into the wet ingredients.

4. Add the wet ingredients to the dry ingredients and stir together until just combined. Do not overmix the batter or the bread will be too dense.

5. Lightly grease a 9 x 5-inch loaf pan and dust it with the almond flour.

6. Spoon the batter in the loaf pan, and bake for about 55 minutes, until a knife inserted in the center comes out clean.

7. Let the loaf cool for about 20 minutes before turning it out onto a wire rack to cool completely before serving.

Makes 1 standard loaf (8–10 slices).

Cranberry and Seed Bread

This pretty bread has a definite crunch from the seeds and satisfying sweetness from the dried fruit. It is an easy energy-packed breakfast or a perfect snack for a pick-me-up throughout the day. The sesame seeds contain amino acids, calcium, and an assortment of minerals. They have a distinctive nutty flavor (especially if you lightly roast them) that provides a pleasing complexity to this bread.

- ¾ cup almond butter, at room temperature
- 4 teaspoons melted coconut oil plus extra to grease loaf pan
- 3 large eggs, lightly beaten
- ¼ cup arrowroot powder
- ½ teaspoon sea salt
- ¼ teaspoon baking soda
- ¾ cup dried cranberries
- ½ cup hulled raw sunflower seeds
- ¼ cup sesame seeds
- ¼ cup pumpkin seeds
- ⅓ cup sliced almonds, divided
- 1 tablespoon almond flour for dusting bread pan

1. Preheat oven to 350 degrees F and lightly grease a 9 x 5-inch loaf pan.

2. In a medium bowl, beat together with a hand mixer or whisk the almond butter, coconut oil, and eggs until the mixture is well blended.

3. In a small bowl, sift together the arrowroot powder, salt, and baking soda.

4. Add the arrowroot mixture to the almond butter mixture and stir until well combined.

5. Gently stir in the cranberries, sunflower seeds, sesame seeds, pumpkin seeds, and the sliced almonds except for 2 tablespoons.

6. Spoon the batter into the loaf pan and top with the remaining sliced almonds.

7. Bake for 40–50 minutes, until a knife inserted into the center comes out clean.

8. Let the loaf cool in the pan for at least 1 hour before serving.

Makes 1 standard loaf (8–10 slices).

Luscious Lemon Bread

This bread is sunshine and summer in one pretty, glazed loaf. It is sweet, tart, and creamy all at the same time. The trick to the pure lemon flavor is to use both the lemon juice and the zest in the bread, as well as a generous splash in the glaze. Follow the instructions carefully to get the correct texture.

For the bread:
- 6 large eggs
- 4 tablespoons melted coconut oil plus extra to grease loaf pan
- Juice and zest from 2 lemons
- ⅔ cup coconut milk, or enough to make 1 cup liquid when added to the lemon juice
- ½ cup honey
- ⅔ cup coconut flour
- 1½ teaspoons baking soda
- ¼ teaspoon sea salt

For the glaze:
- Zest and juice from 1 large lemon
- 2 tablespoons coconut milk
- 4 teaspoons melted coconut oil
- 3 teaspoons honey, or to taste
- ½ teaspoon pure vanilla extract

Make the bread:

1. Preheat oven to 350 degrees F and lightly grease a 9 x 5-inch loaf pan.

2. In a large bowl, whisk together the eggs, coconut oil, lemon zest, lemon juice, coconut milk, and honey until incorporated.

3. In a medium bowl, stir together the coconut flour, baking soda, and salt.

4. Add the dry ingredients to the wet ingredients and stir to combine well.

5. Spoon the batter into the loaf pan and bake for 35–45 minutes, until golden brown and a knife inserted in the center comes out clean.

6. Let the loaf cool for 10 minutes. Then turn it out onto a wire rack until ready to glaze.

Make the glaze:

7. When the lemon loaf comes out of the oven, combine all the ingredients for the glaze in a small saucepan over low heat.

8. Stir constantly until the glaze comes to a simmer. Then remove it from the heat.

9. Cool for at least 15 minutes and then slowly pour over the bread.

10. Place the bread in the refrigerator for at least an hour until the glaze firms up.

Makes 1 standard loaf (8–10 slices).

Sweet Morning Bread

This is an almond-scented loaf sweetened with honey and topped with lightly toasted nuts. What could be nicer than this simple breakfast bread with a cup of tea? If you want to toast this bread, it is better to wait at least until the second day for the loaf to be firm and easy to slice . . . if there is any left!

- 2 cups almond flour
- 2 teaspoons baking powder
- 4 large eggs
- ½ cup melted coconut oil, plus extra to grease loaf pan
- ¼ cup raw honey
- 1 teaspoon almond extract
- ½ cup water
- ½ cup toasted sliced almonds

1. Preheat oven to 350 degrees F and lightly grease a 9 x 5-inch loaf pan.

2. In a medium bowl, combine the almond flour and baking powder.

3. In a large bowl, using an electric mixer, beat the eggs with the coconut oil and honey. Add the almond extract and water, and stir well to combine.

4. Add the flour mixture to the wet ingredients and stir until just combined.

5. Pour the batter into the loaf pan and sprinkle the almond slices over the top.

6. Bake for 30–40 minutes, until a knife inserted into the center comes out clean.

7. Allow the bread to cool completely on a wire rack before removing it from the pan.

Makes 1 standard loaf (8–10 slices).

Grandma's Zucchini Bread

*One of the joys of growing your own zucchini is the bounty of the harvest.
And one of the problems is what to do with the proliferation of squash! This
traditional recipe is a delectable way to use zucchini and create a perfect
afternoon snack or late-evening treat before bed. It is better to leave the skin
on the zucchini when you grate it to add texture to the loaf. Just make sure
to wash the squash well, especially if it is purchased from a store rather
than from your garden.*

- 1½ cups almond flour
- 1 teaspoon baking soda
- 1 teaspoon ground cinnamon
- ½ teaspoon ground nutmeg
- Pinch of ground ginger
- ½ teaspoon sea salt
- 3 large eggs, lightly beaten
- ¼ cup honey
- 1 large ripe banana, mashed
- 1 cup shredded zucchini, squeezed lightly
- Coconut oil to grease the loaf pans

1. Preheat oven to 350 degrees F and lightly grease two 2½ x 4½-inch mini loaf pans.

2. In a medium bowl, stir together the almond flour, baking soda, spices, and salt.

3. In a large bowl whisk together the eggs, honey, banana, and zucchini for about 2 minutes or until very well mixed.

4. Add the dry ingredients to the wet ingredients and stir to combine.

5. Spoon the bread batter into the mini loaf pans.

6. Bake for 30–35 minutes, until a knife comes out clean when inserted in the center.

7. Let the loaves cool for 10 minutes. Then turn it out onto a wire rack until ready to serve.

Makes 2 small loaves (8–10 slices in total).

Date Walnut Bread

If you are looking for a dense, sweet breakfast loaf, this recipe fits that description. Dates are very rich in fiber, calcium, and iron, and eating even one a day contributes to vibrant health. Dates can help regulate digestion, assist with weight control, and contribute to a healthy heart. If you can't find whole dates for this recipe, you can use a prepared paste; however, take care to avoid any products with added sugar or preservatives.

- 1 cup almond flour
- ¼ cup coconut flour
- ½ teaspoon baking soda
- ¼ teaspoon sea salt
- 6 large Medjool dates, pitted
- 6 large eggs
- 2 tablespoons apple cider vinegar
- 1 cup chopped walnuts
- Coconut oil to grease loaf pans

1. Preheat oven to 350 degrees F and lightly grease two 2½ x 4½-inch mini loaf pans.

2. In a food processor, pulse together the almond flour, coconut flour, baking soda, and salt.

3. Add the dates to the processor and pulse until the mixture looks like crumbs.

4. Add the eggs and apple cider vinegar to the other ingredients and pulse to combine.

5. Add the walnuts and pulse a couple times.

6. Transfer the batter to the mini loaf pans.

7. Bake for 30–32 minutes, until a knife inserted in the center comes out clean.

8. Allow the bread to cool for at least 3 hours on a wire rack before removing the loaves from the pans.

Makes 2 small loaves (8–10 slices in total).

Fragrant Pumpkin Bread

Pumpkin is a much loved ingredient in many desserts and breads because the taste is robust, and canned pumpkin is very convenient. The pretty orange color of pumpkin flesh shows this squash is high in beta-carotene, which has been linked to reducing the risk of certain cancers. Pumpkin is also high in vitamins A and C, fiber, potassium, and zinc. Pumpkin also contains L-tryptophan, which can create feelings of well-being and happiness. So this delicious loaf will be a healthy addition to your diet and make you smile!

- 1¼ cups almond flour
- 1½ teaspoons baking soda
- ½ teaspoon ground cinnamon
- ½ teaspoon ground nutmeg
- ¼ teaspoon ground cloves
- Pinch of sea salt
- 3 large eggs

- 1 cup canned unsweetened pumpkin
- ½ cup honey
- ⅓ cup coconut oil, plus extra to grease loaf pan
- 3 tablespoons water, divided
- 2 tablespoons pumpkin seeds

1. Preheat oven to 325 degrees F.

2. In a medium bowl, stir together the almond flour, baking soda, spices, and salt.

3. In a large bowl, whisk the eggs until foamy, about 2 minutes.

4. Whisk in the pumpkin until smooth, and then whisk in the honey and coconut oil.

5. Add about half of the dry ingredients to the pumpkin mixture and stir to combine.

6. Add half the water to the pumpkin mixture and stir to incorporate.

7. Repeat with the rest of the dry ingredients and water until the batter is well blended.

8. Lightly grease a 9 x 5-inch loaf pan and line the bottom with a piece of parchment. Grease the parchment.

9. Spoon the batter into the loaf pan and smooth out the top.

10. Sprinkle with pumpkin seeds and bake for about 1 hour, until a knife inserted into the center comes out clean.

11. Let the loaf cool for 10 minutes. Then turn it out onto a wire rack until completely cool.

Makes 1 standard loaf (8–10 slices).

Tangerine Poppy Seed Bread

This is a tangy sunny loaf that bursts with sweet citrus flavor and the wholesome goodness of tangerines. It can be tricky to zest tangerines because they have thin skins, so use a gentle touch and wash the fruit before zesting or grating. Tangerines are a great source of vitamin C, which is very important for boosting immunity and fighting free radicals that cause cell damage.

- 3½ cups almond flour
- ¼ cup poppy seeds
- ½ teaspoon baking powder
- 5 large eggs
- Juice of 5 tangerines, strained
- Zest of 1 tangerine
- ¼ cup honey
- ¾ tablespoon apple cider vinegar
- Coconut oil to grease loaf pan

1. Preheat oven to 350 degrees F and lightly grease a 9 x 5-inch loaf pan.

2. In a medium bowl, stir together the almond flour, poppy seeds, and baking powder until well combined.

3. In a large bowl, whisk together the eggs, tangerine juice, zest, honey, and apple cider vinegar.

4. Add the dry ingredients to the wet ingredients and mix well.

5. Spoon the batter into the loaf pan.

6. Bake for 40–45 minutes, until a knife inserted in the center comes out clean.

7. Let the loaf cool for 10 minutes. Then turn it out onto a wire rack until ready to serve.

Makes 1 standard loaf (8–10 slices).

Cashew Raisin Bread

This bread is slightly sweet, dense, and simple to make. The maple syrup and cashews are a delectable combination, but this bread needs a little time in the refrigerator to mellow and firm up before slicing. If you don't need slices, then enjoy this bread warm from the oven in chunks.

- 1 cup almond flour
- 1 tablespoon cinnamon
- ½ teaspoon baking soda
- ¼ teaspoon sea salt
- 3 large eggs
- 2 tablespoons pure maple syrup
- 1 teaspoon pure vanilla extract
- ¾ cup chopped cashews
- ½ cup raisins
- Coconut oil to grease loaf pan

1. Preheat oven to 350 degrees F and lightly oil a 9 x 5-inch loaf pan.

2. In a large bowl, stir together all the ingredients except the cashews and raisins until well combined.

3. Gently stir in the cashews and raisins.

4. Lightly oil the loaf pan and line the bottom of the pan with parchment paper.

5. Spoon the batter into the loaf pan.

6. Bake for 35 minutes, until a knife inserted in the center comes out clean.

7. Let the loaf cool for 10 minutes. Then turn it out onto a wire rack until completely cool. Refrigerate for 2 hours or overnight before serving.

Makes 1 standard loaf (8–10 slices).

Cranberry Orange Bread

This pretty loaf is a feast for the eyes as well as the taste buds. It is a lovely golden brown with jewel-like studs of tart cranberry. Cranberries contain powerful antioxidants and vitamin C, which are great for the immune system. Make sure you buy unsweetened dried fruit and not the ones artificially flavored with cherry or strawberry.

- ⅔ cup sifted coconut flour
- 2 teaspoons baking powder
- 1 teaspoon baking soda
- 1 teaspoon sea salt
- Juice of 2 large oranges
- Zest of half an orange

- 2 medium-ripe bananas, mashed
- ¼ cup melted coconut oil plus extra to grease loaf pan
- 4 large eggs, lightly beaten
- 3 tablespoons honey
- ½ cup dried cranberries, roughly chopped

1. Preheat oven to 350 degrees F and lightly grease a 9 x 5-inch loaf pan.

2. In a large bowl, stir together the coconut flour, baking powder, baking soda, and salt until very well combined.

3. In a medium bowl, whisk together the orange juice, orange zest, mashed banana, and coconut oil until blended.

4. Add the eggs and stir to combine.

5. Add the wet ingredients to the dry ingredients and stir to combine.

6. Add the honey and cranberries to the batter and stir to combine.

7. Spoon the batter into the loaf pan and smooth the top.

8. Bake for about 1 hour, until a knife inserted in the center comes out clean.

9. Let the loaf cool for 10 minutes. Then turn it out onto a wire rack until completely cool.

Makes 1 standard loaf (8–10 slices).

Chocolate Raspberry Bread

The finished loaf from this recipe is a tender, golden loaf marbled with chocolate and topped with juicy raspberries. It is what Grandma might have called a "company loaf." You would be proud to serve this to guests, but you also might find yourself hoarding every crumb for yourself. Only use fresh berries or you might find the loaf gets soggy.

- ½ cup coconut flour
- ½ cup flaxseed meal
- 1 teaspoon baking soda
- 2 teaspoons ground cinnamon
- 1 teaspoon sea salt
- 6 large eggs
- 3 large bananas, mashed
- 1 tablespoon pure vanilla extract
- 1 cup fresh raspberries
- 2 tablespoons cocoa powder
- 2 teaspoons coconut milk
- Coconut oil to grease loaf pan

1. Preheat oven to 350 degrees F.

2. In a medium bowl, stir together the coconut flour, flaxseed meal, baking soda, cinnamon, and salt until combined.

3. In a large bowl, beat together the eggs, mashed banana, and vanilla until well blended.

4. Add the dry ingredients in small amounts to the wet ingredients and stir to combine.

5. Spread the fresh raspberries in the bottom of a lightly greased 9 x 5-inch loaf pan, and pour two-thirds of the batter over the raspberries.

6. Add the cocoa powder and coconut milk to the leftover batter and stir to combine.

7. Spoon the chocolate batter over the other batter, and use a knife to swirl the chocolate batter through in a marble pattern.

8. Bake for about 50 minutes, until a knife inserted in the center comes out clean.

9. Allow the bread to cool completely on a wire rack before removing it from the pan. Serve the loaf raspberry side up.

Makes 1 standard loaf (8–10 slices).

Honey Raisin Walnut Bread

Toasted raisin bread is one of life's true pleasures, and this loaf is no exception. Make sure you chill it completely before trying to slice it for toasting, or simply enjoy it warm from the oven. The combination of honey and raisins creates a sweet flavor, so keep that in mind for sandwich toppings. Grilled chicken is absolutely sublime on this bread, especially with a nice olive-oil mayonnaise.

- ¼ cup coconut flour
- 1 teaspoon baking soda
- ¼ teaspoon sea salt
- 5 large eggs
- ½ cup melted coconut oil plus extra to grease loaf pan
- ½ cup honey
- 1 tablespoon pure vanilla extract
- 1 cup raisins
- ½ cup chopped black walnuts

1. Preheat oven to 350 degrees F and lightly grease a 9 x 5-inch loaf pan.

2. In a large bowl, stir together the coconut flour, baking soda, and salt.

3. In a medium bowl, whisk together the eggs, coconut oil, honey, and vanilla until well blended.

4. Add the wet ingredients to the dry ingredients and stir to combine.

5. Stir in the raisins and walnuts.

6. Spoon the batter into the loaf pan and smooth the top.

7. Bake for 50 minutes, until a knife inserted in the center comes out clean.

8. Let the loaf cool for 10 minutes. Then turn it out onto a wire rack until completely cool.

Makes 1 standard loaf (8–10 slices).

Orange Almond Bread

This is a simple recipe bursting with orange, almond, and honey. It is more of a quick bread than a sandwich bread, so serve it topped with a Paleo-friendly jam or on its own right out of the oven. Oranges are known for their vitamin C, but they are also low on the glycemic index and an important part of a heart-healthy diet.

- 3½ cups almond flour
- ½ teaspoon baking powder
- 5 large eggs
- Juice of 2 large oranges, strained
- Zest of 1 orange
- ¼ cup honey
- 1 tablespoon apple cider vinegar
- 2 tablespoons sliced almonds
- Coconut oil to grease loaf pan

1. Preheat oven to 350 degrees F and lightly grease a 9 x 5-inch loaf pan.

2. In a medium bowl, stir together the almond flour and baking powder.

3. In a large bowl, whisk together the eggs, orange juice, orange zest, honey, and apple cider vinegar until well blended.

4. Add the dry ingredients to the wet ingredients and stir to combine.

5. Spoon the batter into the loaf pan and sprinkle the top with almonds.

6. Bake for 40–45 minutes, until a knife inserted in the center comes out clean.

7. Let the loaf cool for 10 minutes. Then turn it out onto a wire rack until completely cool.

Makes 1 standard loaf (8–10 slices).

Coconut Poppy Seed Bread

Coconut flour is a very common ingredient in Paleo breads, and this recipe also includes shredded coconut to enhance the flavor. Coconut is excellent for the immune system, skin, and hair. Eating coconut will also promote very healthy teeth and bones, especially if you shred your own from the actual fruit.

- ¾ cup coconut flour
- 1 teaspoon baking soda
- ¼ teaspoon sea salt
- 4 large eggs, lightly beaten
- ½ cup melted coconut oil, plus extra to grease loaf pan
- ½ cup honey
- 1 teaspoon pure vanilla extract
- ½ cup shredded unsweetened coconut
- ½ cup chopped pecans
- 2 tablespoons poppy seeds

1. Preheat oven to 350 degrees F and lightly grease a 9 x 5-inch loaf pan.

2. In a medium bowl, stir together the coconut flour, baking soda, and salt.

3. In a large bowl, whisk together the eggs, coconut oil, honey, and vanilla until well blended.

4. Add the dry ingredients to the wet ingredients and stir to combine.

5. Stir in the coconut, pecans, and poppy seeds.

6. Spoon the batter into the loaf pan and smooth the top.

7. Bake for 30–40 minutes, until a knife inserted in the center comes out clean.

8. Let the loaf cool for 10 minutes. Then turn it out onto a wire rack until completely cool.

Makes 1 standard loaf (8–10 slices).

Banana Coconut Cardamom Bread

Banana bread is a staple in the Paleo bread repertoire, so it is nice to find a recipe with an unusual variation or ingredient. Cardamom is not the most well-known spice, but once discovered, it might become a favorite. This comes from a plant that is a member of the ginger family, so it should be no surprise that it is pungent and warm. Its exotic flavor combines perfectly with the tropical elements of coconut and banana in this moist loaf.

- 2 cups almond flour
- ⅓ cup coconut flour
- ¼ cup unsweetened shredded coconut, plus extra to sprinkle on loaf
- 1 teaspoon baking soda
- 2 teaspoons ground cardamom
- ¼ teaspoon cinnamon
- ¼ teaspoon nutmeg
- ¼ teaspoon salt
- 2 medium-ripe bananas, mashed
- 4 large eggs
- ¼ cup pure maple syrup
- ¼ cup melted coconut oil, plus extra to grease loaf pan
- 1 tablespoon pure vanilla extract

1. Preheat oven to 325 degrees F and lightly grease a 9 x 5-inch loaf pan.

2. In a medium bowl, stir together the almond flour, coconut flour, shredded coconut, baking soda, spices, and salt until thoroughly combined.

3. In a large bowl, whisk together the mashed banana, eggs, maple syrup, coconut oil, and vanilla until blended.

4. Add the dry ingredients to the wet ingredients and stir to combine.

5. Spoon batter into a loaf pan and sprinkle the top with shredded coconut.

6. Bake for about 45 minutes, until a knife inserted in the center comes out clean.

7. Let the loaf cool for 10 minutes. Then turn it out onto a wire rack until completely cool.

Makes 1 standard loaf (8–10 slices).

Pumpkin Bread with Fresh Blueberries

Pumpkin is used to infuse a richer taste in this pretty berry-studded bread. Pumpkin absorbs flavors easily, so it is a great ingredient for spiced quick breads. Besides being high in beta-carotene, pumpkin is also a natural diuretic, which aids in flushing toxins from the body.

- 1½ cups cashew butter
- 1 cup canned pumpkin puree
- 1 large banana
- 2 large eggs
- 1 cup almond flour
- 2 teaspoons ground cinnamon
- 1 teaspoon baking powder
- 1 teaspoon baking soda
- ¼ teaspoon ground nutmeg
- ¼ teaspoon ground ginger
- Pinch sea salt
- 1 cup fresh blueberries
- Coconut oil to grease the loaf pan

1. Preheat oven to 375 degrees F and lightly grease a 9 x 5-inch loaf pan.

2. In a medium bowl, beat together with a hand mixer or whisk the cashew butter, pumpkin, banana, and eggs until it is a thick and smooth.

3. Add the almond flour, cinnamon, baking powder, baking soda, nutmeg, ginger, and a sea salt, and stir to combine well. Fold the blueberries into the batter.

4. Spoon the batter into the loaf pan and smooth the top.

5. Bake for 45–60 minutes, until a knife inserted in the center comes out clean.

6. Let the loaf cool for 10 minutes. Then turn it out onto a wire rack until ready to serve.

Makes 1 standard loaf (8–10 slices).

Simple Raisin Bread

This recipe is a great starting point for people trying to bake Paleo breads for the first time because it is straightforward but produces a special-tasting loaf of bread. Raisins are a source of boron, which is critical to bone health and the prevention of osteoporosis. They also contain concentrated amounts of polyphenolic phytonutrients, which can help prevent degenerative eye diseases.

- ½ cup flaxseed meal
- ½ cup coconut flour
- ¼ cup arrowroot powder
- 1½ teaspoons baking soda
- 1 teaspoon ground cinnamon
- ½ teaspoon sea salt
- 6 large eggs
- ½ cup unsweetened applesauce
- 2 teaspoons apple cider vinegar
- ¾ cup raisins
- Coconut oil to grease loaf pan

1. Preheat oven to 325 degrees F and lightly grease an 8 x 4-inch loaf pan.

2. In a large bowl, stir together the flaxseed meal, coconut flour, arrowroot powder, baking soda, cinnamon, and sea salt until very well combined.

3. Add the eggs and applesauce, and stir until batter is smooth.

4. Let the batter sit for about 5 minutes, and then stir in the apple cider vinegar and raisins.

5. Spoon the batter into the loaf pan and smooth the top.

6. Bake for 1 hour, until a knife inserted in the center comes out clean.

7. Let the loaf cool for 10 minutes. Then turn it out onto a wire rack until ready to serve.

Makes 1 small loaf (6–8 slices).

Cherry Chocolate-Chip Bread

Tart dried cherries, decadent dark chocolate, ripe bananas, and moist pumpkin puree are mixed together in this recipe to create an exceptional bread that tastes like an indulgence. It will satisfy your cravings for desserts with one bite, and it might become your favorite bread recipe for special occasions and afternoon snacks.

- 1 overripe banana, mashed
- ¼ cup canned pumpkin puree
- 2 tablespoons coconut oil, plus extra to grease loaf pan
- 2 large eggs
- 1 tablespoon raw honey
- 1 tablespoon pure vanilla extract
- 2 cups almond flour
- 1 teaspoon baking soda
- 1 teaspoon baking powder
- ½ teaspoon ground cinnamon
- ½ cup unsweetened dried cherries
- ¼ cup 70-percent-dark chocolate chips

1. Preheat oven to 350 degrees F.

2. In a large bowl, combine the mashed banana, pumpkin puree, and oil. Add the eggs, one at a time, followed by the honey and vanilla, and stir well to combine.

3. In a medium bowl, combine the almond flour, baking soda, baking powder, and cinnamon.

4. Add the flour mixture to the wet ingredients and stir until well combined.

5. Carefully fold in the cherries and chocolate chips.

6. Pour the batter into a lightly greased 9 x 5-inch loaf pan.

7. Bake for 35–40 minutes, until the top of the bread is browned and a knife inserted in the center comes out clean.

8. Allow the bread to cool completely on a wire rack before removing it from the pan.

Makes 1 standard loaf (8–10 slices).

Unforgettable Banana Bread

This recipe creates banana bread that is so marvelous that most people will not guess it is Paleo. Bananas are one of the most Paleo-friendly ingredients in baking, so they are featured in many recipes. Bananas are also a very good choice for anyone looking to follow a healthy lifestyle because they are a great source of many nutrients and vitamins and are high in fiber, potassium, vitamin A, iron, phosphorus, and natural sugars.

- 3 ripe bananas, mashed
- 3 large eggs
- ¼ cup honey
- 3 tablespoons melted coconut oil plus extra to grease loaf pan
- 2 tablespoons coconut cream (the thick layer at the top of a can of coconut milk)
- 1½ cups almond flour
- 3 tablespoons tapioca flour
- 2 tablespoons unsweetened shredded coconut
- 1 teaspoon baking powder
- 1 teaspoon cinnamon
- ½ cup pecan pieces

1. Preheat oven to 325 degrees F.

2. In a large bowl, beat together with a hand mixer or whisk the mashed banana, eggs, honey, coconut oil, and coconut cream until well mixed.

3. In a medium bowl, stir together the remaining ingredients (except the pecans) to combine.

4. Add the dry ingredients to the banana mixture and beat to incorporate.

5. Grease an 8 x 4-inch loaf pan and line the bottom with parchment paper. Grease the parchment as well.

6. Spoon the batter into the loaf pan and smooth the top. Sprinkle with the pecans.

7. Bake for 45 minutes, until a knife inserted in the center comes out clean.

8. Let the loaf cool for 10 minutes. Then turn it out onto a wire rack until completely cool.

Makes 1 small loaf (6–8 slices).

Lime Poppy Seed Bread

This bread is traditionally made with lemons, but limes are a great alternative. Lime is one of the smaller citrus fruits, but it still has significant nutritional benefit, including vitamin C, calcium, iron, and phosphorus. The high vitamin C content can help fight the colds, help in the healing process for cuts, and promote eye, gums, teeth, and bone health.

- 2 cups almond flour
- 2 teaspoons baking powder
- 4 large eggs
- ½ cup melted coconut oil, plus extra to grease loaf pan
- 5 tablespoons raw honey
- Zest of 2 limes
- ½ cup water
- 2 tablespoons poppy seeds

1. Preheat oven to 350 degrees F and lightly grease a 9 x 5-inch loaf pan.

2. In a medium bowl, stir together the flour and baking powder until combined.

3. In a large bowl, using an electric mixer, beat the eggs, coconut oil, and honey. Add the lime zest and water, and stir to combine.

4. Add the flour mixture to the wet ingredients and stir until well combined. Fold in the poppy seeds.

5. Pour the batter into a loaf pan.

6. Bake for 30–40 minutes, until a knife inserted in the center comes out clean.

7. Allow the bread to cool completely on a wire rack before removing it from the pan.

Makes 1 standard loaf (8 to 10 slices).

Spiced Quick Bread

The smell of this bread baking is heavenly, but most people don't realize these spices are also incredibly healthy. Ginger is wonderful for the digestive system and helps alleviate nausea and indigestion. It is also an anti-inflammatory, which can positively impact arthritis and help fight free radicals in the body.

- 2 cups almond flour
- 1 teaspoon baking soda
- 1 tablespoon ground cinnamon
- 1 teaspoon ground ginger
- ½ teaspoon ground cloves
- ¼ teaspoon ground nutmeg
- 2 large eggs
- ½ cup cold water
- 1 teaspoon pure vanilla extract
- ¼ cup pure maple syrup
- ½ cup unsweetened applesauce
- Coconut oil to grease loaf pan

1. Preheat oven to 350 degrees F and lightly grease a 9 x 5-inch loaf pan.

2. In a medium bowl, sift together the almond flour, baking soda, and spices until well combined.

3. In a large bowl, using an electric mixer, beat the eggs until frothy. Add the water, vanilla, and maple syrup, and beat until well combined. Stir in the applesauce and mix well.

4. Carefully add the dry mixture to the wet ingredients and stir until just combined.

5. Pour the batter into the loaf pan, and bake for 35–40 minutes, and spices until the top of the bread is browned and the edges are crisp.

6. Allow the bread to cool completely on a wire rack before removing it from the pan.

Makes 1 standard loaf (8–10 slices).

Pumpkin Bread

When getting the pumpkin for this healthy bread, make sure you choose plain canned pumpkin rather than pie filling, to avoid unhealthy sugars and additives. If you have time, you can even roast your own little pumpkin in the oven and use the scooped out flesh for a truly spectacular depth of taste. Make sure you let the pumpkin cool down before beating it together with your eggs, or the eggs will cook instead of blend!

- 1 cup almond flour
- 1 teaspoon baking soda
- 2 teaspoons ground cinnamon
- ¼ teaspoon ground nutmeg
- ¼ teaspoon ground cloves
- ½ cup pumpkin puree (canned or freshly roasted)
- 3 tablespoons raw honey
- 3 large eggs
- Coconut oil to grease loaf pan

1. Preheat oven to 350 degrees F. Grease a 9 x 5-inch loaf pan with coconut oil and set aside.

2. In a medium bowl, stir together the almond flour, baking soda, cinnamon, nutmeg, and cloves.

3. In a large bowl, using an electric mixer beat the pumpkin puree, honey, and eggs until frothy.

4. Carefully add the dry mixture to the wet ingredients and stir until just combined.

5. Pour the batter into the loaf pan, and bake for 30–40 minutes, until the top of the bread is lightly browned and a knife inserted into the center comes out clean.

6. Allow the bread to cool completely on a wire rack before removing it from the pan. Slice and serve.

7. Store any leftover slices in an airtight container or wrapped in plastic wrap for up to 3 days.

Makes 1 loaf (8–10 slices).

Hearty Maple Walnut Bread

If you are a French toast fan, this will be your new favorite Paleo bread. The crunch of walnuts, sweetness of maple syrup, and moistness from the ripe bananas all combine together in this delectable loaf. This bread, unfortunately, is not one to try hot from the oven because it needs to be completely cool to slice easily. Have patience, though — it is worth it!

- 2 cups almond flour
- 1 tablespoon ground cinnamon
- 1 teaspoon baking soda
- 2 large eggs
- ½ cup cold water
- 1 teaspoon pure vanilla extract
- ¼ cup pure maple syrup
- 2 overripe bananas, mashed
- 1 cup chopped walnuts, divided
- Coconut oil to grease loaf pan

1. Preheat oven to 350 degrees F and lightly grease a 9 x 5-inch loaf pan.

2. In a medium bowl, sift together the almond flour, cinnamon, and baking soda until well combined.

3. In a large bowl, using an electric mixer, beat the eggs until light yellow and frothy. Add the water, vanilla, and maple syrup, and beat until well combined.

4. Stir in the mashed banana, and then fold in ½ cup of the chopped walnuts.

5. Carefully add the dry mixture to the wet ingredients and stir until just combined.

6. Pour the batter into the loaf pan, sprinkle with the remaining walnuts, and bake for 35–40 minutes, until the top of the bread is browned and the edges are crisp.

7. Allow the bread to cool completely on a wire rack before removing it from the pan.

Makes 1 standard loaf (8–10 slices).

Spiced Applesauce Bread

Many non-Paleo bread recipes use applesauce as a base ingredient because it adds moistness, flavor, and texture to the finished loaf. This recipe makes applesauce the star. This loaf should be made with unsweetened applesauce (homemade, if possible) for the best results.

- 2 cups almond flour
- 1 tablespoon ground cinnamon
- 1 teaspoon baking soda
- 2 large eggs
- ½ cup cold water
- ¼ cup pure maple syrup
- 1 teaspoon pure vanilla extract
- ½ cup unsweetened applesauce
- 1 large apple, peeled, cored, and chopped
- ¼ cup chopped pecans
- Coconut oil to grease loaf pan

1. Preheat oven to 350 degrees F and lightly grease a 9 x 5-inch loaf pan.

2. In a medium bowl, sift together the almond flour, cinnamon, and baking soda until well combined.

3. In a large bowl, using an electric mixer, beat the eggs until frothy. Add the water, maple syrup, and vanilla, and stir until well combined. Stir in the applesauce, and then fold in the chopped apple.

4. Carefully add the flour mixture to the wet ingredients and stir until just combined.

5. Pour the batter into the loaf pan and sprinkle the pecans over the top.

6. Bake for 35–40 minutes, until the top of the bread is browned and the edges are crisp.

7. Allow the bread to cool completely on a wire rack before removing it from the pan.

Makes 1 standard loaf (8–10 slices).

Bread is the warmest, kindest of all words. Write it always with a capital letter, like your own name.

—Anonymous

4

FLATBREADS, ROLLS, MUFFINS, AND PIZZA DOUGH

Garlic Breadsticks with Oregano

This recipe is a perfect place to use any leftover bacon fat as long as you strain out any floating solid bits before using it. The hint of bacon, garlic, and oregano combine together for a rich taste experience. You might find the dough can sometimes pull apart when you are placing it on the baking sheet. Simply stick the broken piece back on and pinch to seal. These don't have to look perfect to be delicious!

- ¼ cup water
- 4 tablespoons canned coconut milk
- 2 tablespoons bacon fat
- ½ teaspoon sea salt
- 1½ cups tapioca flour
- 1 large egg, beaten
- 3 teaspoons minced garlic
- 3 tablespoons minced fresh oregano
- Sea salt for sprinkling

1. Preheat oven to 500 degrees F.

2. Combine the water, coconut milk, bacon fat, and sea salt in a small saucepan, and bring to a simmer over medium heat.

3. Place the tapioca flour in a large bowl and make a well in the center. Pour the liquid into the middle. Stir to combine, and then let the dough sit for about 10 minutes to allow it to come to room temperature.

4. Add the egg, garlic, and oregano to the dough, and mix it in with your hands.

5. Separate the dough into eight equal pieces.

6. Take a piece of dough, and stretch it across a parchment-paper-lined baking sheet into a basic breadstick shape. The dough might rip—simply stick the piece back on. Flatten the dough out using your fingertips. Repeat with remaining dough.

7. Sprinkle the breadsticks with sea salt, and bake for about 10 minutes. Serve warm.

Makes 8 breadsticks.

Paleo Tortillas

Making your own Paleo tortillas is surprisingly easy and requires very few ingredients. The trick to great tortillas lies in the rolling-out step of the process. You must get the dough very thin without tearing it to get the right texture and thinness to use these for wraps and enchiladas. A little cumin or cayenne in the batter can also be a tasty addition, especially if you like spicy food.

• 2 cups of almond flour	• Water, if needed
• 2 large eggs, lightly beaten	• 3 tablespoons extra-virgin olive oil, or as needed for frying
• 1 teaspoon melted coconut oil	
• ¼ teaspoon salt (or to taste)	

1. Combine the almond flour, eggs, coconut oil, and salt in a medium bowl until well mixed.

2. Gather the dough into a ball and knead using the sides of the bowl until the dough is elastic. Add a little water if the dough is too dry.

3. Divide the dough in four to six equal balls, and roll out each ball thinly between two pieces of parchment paper.

4. Heat the olive oil in a frying pan over medium heat and fry each tortilla, turning once until cooked, about 30 seconds a side.

5. Remove tortillas from the pan and place on paper towels to drain.

6. Repeat until all the tortillas are cooked.

7. Serve warm, wrapped around a favorite filling.

Makes 4–6 tortillas, depending on the size.

Italian Garlic Buns

If you want a change from using bread for your sandwich and soup dipping needs, these buns are a nice alternative. They have a heavenly scent and the texture is quite light for a nonyeast creation. It is best to use fresh minced garlic in this recipe rather than powder.

- ¾ cup tapioca flour
- ¼ cup coconut flour
- ½ teaspoon sea salt
- ½ teaspoon chopped fresh oregano
- ½ teaspoon chopped fresh basil
- ½ cup coconut oil, plus extra to grease baking sheet
- ½ cup water
- 1 teaspoon minced garlic
- 1 large egg, lightly beaten

1. Preheat oven to 350 degrees F and lightly grease a baking sheet.

2. In a medium bowl, stir together the tapioca flour, coconut flour, salt, and herbs.

3. In a small saucepan, heat the coconut oil and water together until scalding.

4. Remove from heat and add the garlic to the pan. Set aside for at least 10 minutes.

5. Add the oil mixture to the dry ingredients and stir to combine. Add the egg and mix thoroughly.

6. Gather the dough into a ball and knead for about 2–3 minutes. Then divide into 1½-inch balls and place on baking sheet.

7. Bake for 35–40 minutes and serve warm.

Makes about 12 buns, depending on the size.

Paleo Herbed Pizza Dough

If you are on a Paleo diet, one of the hardest things to give up is pizza. That's why this recipe will quickly become a staple in your household. The finished crust is crisp and easy to cut as long as you don't overload it with toppings. If you want a chewier crust, keep it a little thicker when pressing it in the pizza pan.

- 1²/₃ cups almond flour
- ½ cup arrowroot powder
- 2 teaspoons minced garlic
- ½ teaspoon baking soda
- 1 teaspoon sea salt
- 2 large eggs
- 4 teaspoons extra-virgin olive oil
- 1 teaspoon chopped fresh rosemary
- 1 teaspoon chopped fresh oregano

1. Preheat oven to 350 degrees F.

2. In a large bowl, stir together almond flour, arrowroot powder, garlic, baking soda, and salt.

3. In a small bowl, whisk the eggs and oil together with the herbs.

4. Add the wet ingredients to the dry ingredients and mix well until the batter forms into a ball. Add more almond flour if the dough is too wet.

5. Press the dough onto a 12-inch pizza pan or form a rough circle on a baking sheet. Crimp the edges slightly to create a lip all the way around.

6. Top with desired toppings and bake for about 20 minutes or until crisp.

Makes one 12-inch pizza crust.

Fresh Herb Focaccia

Focaccia is a popular flatbread that is used as a snack and sandwich base. This recipe uses Greek yogurt, which some Paleo purists feel should be avoided; however, it can be eaten in moderation. Greek yogurt is considered to be one of the healthiest foods in the world, so giving it a try can be beneficial.

- ¼ cup coconut flour
- ¼ cup flaxseed meal
- ¼ teaspoon baking soda
- ¼ teaspoon sea salt
- 4 large eggs
- ⅓ cup Greek yogurt
- 1 teaspoon honey

- 1 teaspoon chopped fresh thyme
- 1 teaspoon chopped fresh rosemary
- 1 tablespoon extra-virgin olive oil, or to taste
- Sea salt, to taste

---

1. Preheat oven to 375 degrees F.

2. In a large bowl, stir together the coconut flour, flaxseed meal, baking soda, and salt.

3. In a medium bowl, whisk together the eggs, Greek yogurt, and honey until smooth.

4. Add the wet ingredients to the dry ingredients and stir to combine. Set aside for 2 minutes.

5. Using a spatula, spread the batter evenly onto a parchment-paper-lined baking sheet until it is about ¾ inch thick.

6. Sprinkle the batter with the thyme and the rosemary, taking care to distribute the herbs evenly.

7. Bake for 10–12 minutes.

8. Remove from the oven, drizzle with the olive oil, and sprinkle with sea salt. Serve warm.

Makes 1 large focaccia bread.

Golden Dinner Rolls

A good dinner roll can be the perfect addition to a nice roast beef or chicken dinner, especially when you are entertaining. This recipe does take a bit of creative measuring with regard to the coconut flour so that the dough does not end up too dry. When you add the coconut flour, do so in small amounts and let the dough sit for a few minutes between additions so it has a chance to absorb the flour.

- 1½ cups tapioca flour
- 1½ teaspoons sea salt
- ½–⅔ cup coconut flour
- ¾ cup extra-virgin olive oil
- ¾ cup warm water
- 2 small eggs, lightly beaten

1. Preheat oven to 350 degrees F.

2. In a large bowl, stir together the tapioca flour and salt with about ½ cup of coconut flour to start.

3. In a small bowl, whisk together the olive oil, water, and eggs, and pour mixture into the dry ingredients.

4. Stir until combined. If the dough is too loose and thin, add more coconut flour until you have a soft dough that is still a little sticky.

5. Use a spoon to scoop out portions of dough and roll them into 2-inch balls.

6. Place the dough balls on a parchment-paper-lined baking sheet.

7. Bake for about 35 minutes, until lightly golden. Serve warm.

Makes 10 dinner rolls.

Old-Fashioned Soft Pretzels

These salty pretzels are amazing right out of the oven or served at room temperature with a Paleo-friendly dip. Part of the fun of making these treats is learning to twist them into the traditional pretzel shape. Your first few pretzels might not look perfect, but bake them anyway because they will taste delicious no matter what they look like! You can experiment with flavored finishing salts to create different variations, such as Himalayan pink or smoked salt.

- ½ cup extra-virgin olive oil, plus extra to brush pretzels
- ½ cup of water
- 2 tablespoons apple cider vinegar
- 2 teaspoons of sea salt, divided

- ½ cup of tapioca flour
- ½ teaspoon baking powder
- ½ teaspoon baking soda
- 1 cup coconut flour
- 1 egg, lightly beaten

---

1. Preheat oven to 350 degrees F.

2. Place the olive oil, water, apple cider vinegar, and ½ teaspoon of the salt in a medium saucepan, and bring to a boil over medium heat.

3. Remove from the heat and add the tapioca flour. Stir to combine. Add the baking powder and baking soda to the mixture and stir. The mixture will foam. Add the coconut flour and egg, and mix until a firm dough forms.

4. Turn the dough out onto a work surface lightly dusted with tapioca flour, and knead the dough for 2–5 minutes.

5. Pinch off a 2-inch piece of dough and roll it into a thin snake about 6 inches long. Twist the log into a traditional pretzel shape. (This might take a little practice.) Place the pretzel on a

parchment-paper-lined baking sheet. Repeat until all the dough is used up.

6. Brush the pretzels with a little olive oil, and sprinkle sea salt over them. Bake for 25–30 minutes, until golden. Serve warm whenever possible.

Makes about 18 pretzels.

Paleo Sandwich Buns

One of the things many people miss when starting a Paleo diet is crusty, airy rolls to dip into soup or use to make sandwiches. These buns are not as crusty as a ciabatta or as kaiser rolls, but they do use yeast, which creates a nice, light texture and rise. If you want bigger buns, spoon the batter into giant silicone muffin cups instead of the standard-sized tins.

- ⅓ cup full-fat canned coconut milk
- ¼ cup honey
- 1 package active dry yeast
- 6 large eggs
- ⅓ cup coconut oil, plus extra to grease muffin tins
- ½ cup flaxseed meal
- ½ cup coconut flour
- 1 teaspoon baking soda
- 1 teaspoon sea salt

1. Combine the coconut milk and honey in a small saucepan, and heat until the mixture reaches 105–115 degrees F.

2. Pour the mixture into a large bowl and sprinkle with the yeast. Let this sit until the yeast gets foamy, about 10 minutes.

3. Add the eggs and coconut oil to the yeast mixture, and stir to combine. Add the flaxseed meal, coconut flour, baking soda, and salt to the yeast mixture, and stir to blend well.

4. Cover the bowl with a clean kitchen towel, and place in a warm spot for about 1½–2 hours to let the batter rise.

5. Stir the batter until it is the same starting volume, and then spoon evenly into lightly greased muffin tins.

6. Cover the tins with a clean cloth, and let the batter rise again for about 40 minutes or until double in size.

7. Preheat oven to 350 degrees F.

8. Bake for 15–20 minutes, until golden on top.

9. Let cool for about 5 minutes and pop the buns out of the muffin tin. Serve piping hot or at room temperature.

Makes 12 buns.

Tasty Breadsticks

If you really love breadsticks, the length of this recipe will not dissuade you from making these garlicky treats. Make sure you follow the directions to the letter to get the best results. The finished breadsticks actually taste very close to non-Paleo versions, and the texture is exceptional. You could use fresh garlic instead of powdered to create an even stronger flavor, but try the original recipe first to see if it suits your palate. Fresh garlic can scorch if it is not small enough or mixed thoroughly into the batter. This creates a very unpleasant, bitter taste.

For the breadsticks:
- 1½ cups almond flour
- 1 teaspoon dried oregano
- ½ teaspoon dried basil
- ½ teaspoon sea salt
- ¼ teaspoon garlic powder
- 1 tablespoon extra-virgin olive oil
- 2 large eggs, beaten
- 2 tablespoons coconut flour, divided

For the topping:
- 1 large egg
- 1 teaspoon water
- ½ teaspoon dried basil
- ½ teaspoon sea salt
- ¼ teaspoon garlic powder

Make the breadsticks:

1. Preheat oven to 350 degrees F.

2. In a medium bowl, stir together almond flour, oregano, basil, sea salt, garlic powder, olive oil, and eggs until combined. Let the dough set for several minutes, and then add about 1 tablespoon of the coconut flour, stirring to mix.

3. Let the dough sit again so the coconut flour can dry it out, and then add the remaining 1 tablespoon of coconut flour. Stir to combine, and roll the dough into a ball. Divide the ball into 4 equal pieces.

4. On a clean work surface, roll 1 piece of dough into a long snake about ½-inch thick. Fold the snake in half so there are two equal pieces the same length lying side by side.

5. Pinch the two ends together on both ends and twist the two pieces together carefully to form a twisty rope. Place on a parchment-paper-lined baking sheet. Repeat with the remaining pieces.

6. Bake for about 10 minutes and then remove from the oven.

Make the topping:

7. While the breadsticks are baking, in a small bowl, whisk together the egg and water.

8. In a small cup, toss together the basil, sea salt, and garlic powder.

9. Once the breadsticks have been removed from the oven (see step 6 above), flip them over with a spatula.

10. Brush the tops of the breadsticks with the egg wash and then sprinkle with the herb mix.

11. Return the breadsticks to the oven and bake for an additional 5 minutes. Allow the breadsticks to cool for 2–5 minutes before serving.

Makes 4 breadsticks.

Paleo Flatbread

This is more a naan bread than a flatbread, and it should be eaten, whenever possible, warm and tender right after cooking. The trick to pliable golden flatbreads is applying a nice, even coat of coconut oil in your skillet before cooking each one. If your pan isn't evenly coated with oil, the bread will be too crispy and won't be hollow inside.

- ⅓ cup tapioca flour
- ¼ cup coconut flour
- 1 teaspoon baking powder
- ½ teaspoon sea salt
- ½ teaspoon garlic powder
- ¼ teaspoon onion powder
- 12 large egg whites
- ½ cup water
- 2 tablespoons apple cider vinegar
- 1 tablespoon honey
- Coconut oil for frying

1. In a large bowl, stir together the tapioca flour, coconut flour, baking powder, salt, garlic powder, and onion powder until very well combined.

2. Add the other ingredients except the coconut oil, and stir until a thin batter forms.

3. Place a skillet over low heat and brush the bottom with melted coconut oil using a pastry brush. You should create a thin coating that reaches to the edges of the skillet.

4. Use a small ladle to add about ¼ cup of batter to the center of the skillet, and spread the batter to the size you want the flatbreads.

5. Fry until firm and lightly browned on the bottom, and then flip it over and cook the other side until it is also lightly browned.

6. Remove the flatbread from the skillet and place it on a plate.

7. Brush the skillet with oil again and repeat until all the batter is used up.

Makes 10 flatbreads.

Simple Paleo Pizza Dough

This is a very simple recipe that will make two medium-sized crusts for all your pizza cravings. The best part of this dough is that it freezes well and bakes up quite crispy. If you are a thin-crust enthusiast, you will like its texture and crunch.

- 3 large eggs
- 2 cups almond flour
- ¼ cup coconut flour
- 2 tablespoons melted coconut oil
- 1 tablespoon water

1. Preheat oven to 400 degrees F.

2. In a medium bowl, using an electric mixer, beat the eggs until light yellow and frothy.

3. In a large bowl, stir together the almond and coconut flours and coconut oil until well combined. Stir in the water.

4. Add the eggs to the flour mixture and stir until well combined. Allow the dough to rest for 5 minutes, and then stir again, adding a little more water if necessary to make the dough pliable and easy to knead. The dough should be lightly sticky, but not wet. Allow the dough to rest for 5 more minutes.

5. Divide the dough into two equal pieces. Lightly knead each piece into a ball, dusting with a little almond flour if necessary to keep the dough soft. Roll out to desired thickness.

6. Top the dough as desired, place directly on a pizza stone or pizza pan, and bake until the crust edges are lightly browned and crisp.

Makes 2 medium-sized pizza crusts.

Old-Fashioned Cinnamon Rolls

Cinnamon rolls have garnered a bad reputation as fatty, calorie-laden, sugar-drenched treats that should be avoided at all costs. This can be true of some cinnamon rolls, but not the ones made using this Paleo-inspired recipe. These rolls are sweet, tender, and absolutely perfect for a leisurely Sunday morning spent with loved ones. Try to eat them warm from the oven, or if you have leftovers, pop them in the microwave for a few seconds.

For the dough:
- 2 large eggs
- 1 tablespoon raw honey
- ¼ cup coconut oil plus 2 tablespoons, divided
- 2 cups almond flour
- 1 teaspoon baking soda
- 2 tablespoons ground cinnamon
- 3 tablespoons coconut sugar
- ½ cup coarsely chopped pecans

For the icing:
- ¼ cup full-fat canned coconut milk
- ¼ cup coconut sugar
- 1 tablespoon pure vanilla extract
- 1 teaspoon arrowroot powder

Make the dough:

1. Preheat oven to 350 degrees F.

2. In a large bowl, using an electric mixer, beat the eggs and honey. Add ¼ cup of coconut oil and stir to combine.

3. In a medium bowl, stir together the almond flour and baking soda. Add the flour mixture to the wet ingredients, and stir until a stiff dough forms.

4. Lay a large piece of parchment paper on a clean surface and place the dough on it. Lay another piece of parchment on top, and then roll out the dough until you have a rectangle about ¼-inch thick.

5. In a small bowl, combine the 2 tablespoons of coconut oil, cinnamon, and sugar. Sprinkle over the rolled-out dough. Then sprinkle with the chopped pecans.

6. Roll up the dough, starting with the longer side of the rectangle, and slice into eight to ten (2-inch-thick) cinnamon rolls. Position the rolls on a parchment-paper-lined baking sheet.

7. Bake for 15–20 minutes, until the rolls are lightly browned.

For the icing:
8. In a small bowl, stir together the coconut milk, sugar, vanilla, and arrowroot powder until well combined.

9. Using a spoon or spatula, drizzle the icing over the warm cinnamon rolls and serve warm.

Makes about 8 rolls.

Flaxseed Focaccia

Flaxseeds are used a great deal in Paleo bread recipes because they almost mimic the texture of wheat flour when they are ground up. This flatbread has a distinctive nutty taste from the flaxseeds and almond butter, which helps this bread complement Asian marinated chicken and pork. You can even make this the day before and grill it lightly (to reheat) alongside your main protein.

- 1 cup ground flaxseed
- ¼ cup almond flour
- 1 teaspoon baking soda
- ¾ cup raw almond butter
- 1 tablespoon raw honey
- 3 large eggs
- 3 tablespoons extra-virgin olive oil

1. Preheat oven to 350 degrees F.

2. In a small bowl, stir together the flaxseed, almond flour, and baking soda until combined.

3. In a large bowl, combine the almond butter and honey. Add in the eggs, one at a time, stirring between each addition.

4. Add the flour mixture to the wet ingredients and stir until a wet dough forms.

5. Line a 9 x 13-inch jelly-roll pan with parchment paper, and drizzle the olive oil on the parchment. Then spread the dough over it. Allow the dough to rest for 5 minutes.

6. Bake for 25–30 minutes, until the top of the focaccia is golden brown. Allow the bread to cool.

Makes 8–10 servings.

Rosemary Flatbread

Flatbreads are a great choice for new bakers to try out their bread-making skills because they don't require any fancy techniques or even a loaf pan. Rosemary is a truly lovely addition to this bread because it goes with almost any accompanying dish or is marvelous on its own with a little dish of olive oil for dipping.

- ¼ cup almond flour
- ¼ cup arrowroot powder
- 1 teaspoon baking soda
- ¾ cup raw almond butter
- 1 tablespoon raw honey
- 3 large eggs
- 2 tablespoons finely chopped rosemary
- 3 tablespoons extra-virgin olive oil
- Coarse sea salt for topping (optional)

1. Preheat oven to 350 degrees F.

2. In a small bowl, stir together the almond flour, arrowroot powder, and baking soda until combined.

3. In a large bowl, combine the almond butter and honey. Add the eggs, one at a time, stirring between each addition. Stir in the rosemary.

4. Add the flour mixture to the wet ingredients and stir until a wet dough forms.

5. Line a 9 x 13-inch jelly-roll pan with parchment paper, and drizzle the olive oil on the parchment. Then spread the dough over it. Allow the dough to rest for 5 minutes.

6. Bake for 25 to 30 minutes, until the top of the bread is golden brown.

7. Top with sea salt if desired. Allow the bread to cool.

Makes 12 servings.

Savory Herb Dinner Rolls

Stews, hearty soups, rich gravy, and casseroles would all benefit from sharing the plate (or bowl) with these savory rolls. These dinner rolls are simple to make and feature a hint of honey. They can be made in advance and warmed up wrapped in a clean kitchen cloth in a low oven if you are time challenged. Enjoy!

- 3 large eggs
- 1 tablespoon raw honey
- 1 tablespoon water
- 2 tablespoons coconut oil, plus extra to grease cake pan
- 2 cups almond flour
- ¼ cup coconut flour
- 1 cup ground flaxseed
- 1 tablespoon ground dill
- 1 teaspoon onion powder
- 1 teaspoon baking soda

1. Preheat oven to 400 degrees F.

2. In a medium bowl, using an electric mixer, beat the eggs until light yellow and frothy. Add the honey, water, and coconut oil, and stir to combine.

3. In a large bowl, stir together the almond and coconut flours, flaxseed, dill, onion powder, and baking soda until well combined.

4. Add the egg mixture to the dry ingredients and stir until well combined.

5. Allow the dough to rest for 5 minutes, and then stir again, adding a little more water if necessary to make the dough pliable and easy to knead. The dough should be lightly sticky but not wet. Allow the dough to rest for 5 more minutes.

6. Divide the dough into twelve equal pieces. Lightly knead each piece of dough into a ball, dusting with a little almond flour if necessary to keep the dough soft. Nestle the dough rolls into a lightly greased, 9-inch round cake pan.

7. Bake for 20–25 minutes, until the tops of the rolls are browned.

Makes 12 rolls.

Hearty Breakfast Muffins

Mornings can be hectic, and a healthy breakfast is often forgotten in the rush to get out the door. This is a fast recipe that delivers crunch, texture, sweetness, and lots of fiber. You can make a big batch of these and freeze them individually for a quick grab when you need a healthy start.

- ½ cup coconut flour
- ¼ cup ground flaxseed
- 2 teaspoons baking powder
- 6 large eggs

- ½ cup coconut oil, plus extra to grease muffin pan
- ½ cup chopped pecans, toasted if desired
- ½ cup dried cranberries

---

1. Preheat oven to 350 degrees F.

2. In a medium bowl, stir together the coconut flour, flaxseed, and baking powder until combined.

3. In a large bowl, using an electric mixer, beat the eggs and coconut oil. Add the flour mixture to the wet ingredients and stir until well combined.

4. Gently fold in the pecans and cranberries.

5. Spoon the batter into a lightly greased muffin pan, filling each cup about halfway.

6. Bake for 12–15 minutes, until the muffin tops are lightly browned.

7. Allow the muffins to cool for 10 minutes before removing from the pan.

Makes 12 muffins.

Tender "Buttermilk" Biscuits

True Southern-style biscuits are a thing of beauty, especially when pulled open to release fragrant buttery steam. These Paleo-friendly biscuits are a pretty fair substitute without the wheat. Try them on Sunday morning topped with sliced ham and a neatly poached egg or alongside a festive roasted turkey on a special occasion.

- 6 large egg whites
- ½ cup coconut milk
- ¼ teaspoon apple cider vinegar
- 1½ cups almond flour
- ¼ cup coconut flour
- 2 teaspoons baking powder
- 2 tablespoons chilled coconut oil

1. Preheat oven to 350 degrees F.

2. In a medium bowl, using an electric mixer, beat the egg whites, coconut milk, and apple cider vinegar until well combined.

3. In a large bowl, stir together the almond and coconut flours and baking powder until combined. Add the cold coconut oil and mix with a fork until the mixture resembles coarse crumbs.

4. Add the egg mixture to the dry ingredients and stir until a wet dough forms.

5. Using an ice-cream scoop, scoop rounded portions of the dough onto a parchment-paper-lined baking sheet.

6. Bake for 10–15 minutes, until the tops of the biscuits are lightly browned. Allow the biscuits to cool for a few minutes before serving.

Makes 8 biscuits.

Light "Buttermilk" Pancakes

Buttermilk is one of those ingredients that some people include in their Paleo diet and others do not. This recipe assumes the latter and uses coconut milk with vinegar to mimic the tart buttermilk flavor. If you do incorporate real buttermilk in your meals, then simply swap the coconut milk and vinegar for an equal measure of buttermilk. You can make extra pancakes using this recipe and enjoy them cold with a bit of Paleo jam for a nice snack.

- ¼ cup coconut flour
- ¼ cup almond flour
- ½ teaspoon baking soda
- ¼ teaspoon salt
- 4 large eggs, lightly beaten

- ¼ cup coconut oil plus extra to grease skillet
- ¼ cup coconut milk
- 1 teaspoon honey
- 1 teaspoon pure vanilla extract
- ¼ teaspoon apple cider vinegar

---

1. In a large bowl, stir together the coconut and almond flours, baking soda, and salt until well combined.

2. Stir in the eggs, coconut oil, coconut milk, honey, vanilla, and apple cider vinegar until batter is well blended.

3. Heat a skillet over medium-low heat and add a little coconut oil.

4. Ladle the pancake batter into the skillet and cook until the bottom is golden. Then flip the pancake over and cook the second side. Repeat until all the batter is used up.

Makes 8–10 pancakes.

Tender "Cream" Scones

Scones are a traditional accompaniment for afternoon tea or a steaming mug of coffee in the morning. These lightly golden scones are moist and tender without the addition of heavy cream and sugar. You can even dress this recipe up with hazelnuts, dark chocolate chips, raisins, and a hint of lemon if you are feeling creative.

- 6 large egg whites
- ½ cup canned full-fat coconut milk
- 1½ cups almond flour
- ¼ cup coconut flour
- 2 teaspoons baking powder
- 2 tablespoons chilled coconut oil

1. Preheat oven to 350 degrees F.

2. In a medium bowl, using an electric mixer, beat the egg whites and coconut milk until combined.

3. In a large bowl, stir together the almond and coconut flours and baking powder until combined. Add the cold coconut oil and mix with a fork until the mixture resembles coarse crumbs.

4. Add the egg mixture to the dry ingredients and stir until a wet dough forms.

5. Using an ice-cream scoop, scoop rounded portions of the dough onto a parchment-paper-lined baking sheet.

6. Bake for 10–15 minutes, until the tops of the scones are lightly browned. Allow the scones to cool for a few minutes before serving.

Makes 8 scones.

Harvest Dinner Rolls

Golden rolls piled in a pretty cloth-lined basket are a traditional part of many dinner tables all over the world. These rolls have a sweetness that comes from pumpkin, and you can easily double this recipe if your gathering is large or you want to freeze a batch for later use.

- 3 large eggs
- ½ cup pumpkin puree (canned or freshly roasted)
- 2 cups almond flour
- ¼ cup coconut flour
- 2 tablespoons melted coconut oil, plus extra to grease cake pan
- 1 tablespoon water

1. Preheat oven to 400 degrees F.

2. In a medium bowl, using an electric mixer, beat the eggs until light yellow and frothy. Add the pumpkin puree and stir until well combined.

3. In a large bowl, stir together the almond and coconut flours and coconut oil until well combined. Stir in the water.

4. Add the egg mixture to the flour mixture and stir until well combined.

5. Allow the dough to rest for 5 minutes, then stir again, adding a little more water if necessary to make the dough pliable and easy to knead.

6. The dough should be lightly sticky, but not wet. Allow the dough to rest for 5 more minutes.

7. Divide the dough into twelve equal pieces. Lightly knead each piece of dough into a ball, dusting with a little almond flour if necessary to keep the dough soft. Nestle the dough rolls into a lightly greased, 9-inch round cake pan.

8. Bake for 20–25 minutes, until the tops of the rolls are browned.

Makes 12 rolls.

Blueberry Muffins

This is a very cakey, lightly sweetened muffin that's bursting with fresh berries and a subtle almond taste. If you have to use frozen berries instead of fresh, put them in frozen so you don't end up with blue-tinted muffins. Blueberries are a wonderful addition to a healthy breakfast or snack because they have the highest total antioxidant capacity. This means they are a strong disease-fighting food.

- 2 cups almond flour
- ¼ teaspoon baking soda
- ⅛ teaspoon sea salt
- ¼ cup honey
- 1 cup full-fat canned coconut milk
- ¼ cup melted coconut oil
- 2 large eggs
- ¾ cup fresh blueberries

1. Preheat oven to 350 degrees F.

2. In a large bowl, stir together the almond flour, baking soda, and salt until well mixed.

3. In a medium bowl, stir together the honey, coconut milk, coconut oil, and eggs, until well blended.

4. Add the wet ingredients to the almond flour mixture and stir to combine.

5. Fold the blueberries into the batter carefully.

6. Fill paper-lined muffin tins with batter about two-thirds full.

7. Bake for 20–25 minutes, until golden brown.

8. Let muffins cool completely before removing them from the pan.

Makes 12 muffins.

Chocolate Banana Muffins

These are almost like having dessert for breakfast. Make sure you use very good quality 70-percent dark chocolate to stay within the Paleo guidelines and get the full health benefits. Dark chocolate is heart healthy, has a positive effect on mood, and helps control blood sugar. If you can't find chips that are dark, try to get a chocolate bar and chop it yourself.

- 3 large ripe bananas, mashed
- 3 large eggs
- ¼ cup melted coconut oil
- ¼ cup honey
- ⅓ cup cocoa powder
- 3 tablespoons coconut flour
- ¼ teaspoon baking soda
- ¼ teaspoon salt
- ⅓ cup dark-chocolate chips

1. Preheat oven to 350 degrees F.

2. In a medium bowl, stir together the mashed bananas, eggs, coconut oil, and honey until well blended.

3. Add the cocoa powder, coconut flour, baking soda, and salt and stir to combine.

4. Fill paper-lined muffin tins with batter about two-thirds full. Sprinkle tops with chocolate chips.

5. Bake for approximately 15–20 minutes.

6. Cool completely and serve.

Makes 10 muffins.

The smell of good bread baking, like the sound of lightly flowing water, is indescribable in its evocation of innocence and delight.

—M. F. K. Fisher

5

PALEO DIET BASICS

Whether modern health care professionals want to admit it or not, the Paleo diet closely mirrors what most of them tell their patients: Eat more fruits, vegetables, and lean meats, and stay away from processed garbage. The diet, also known as the Stone Age diet, the caveman diet, and the hunter-gatherer diet, has gained a significant following in recent years, and there's some pretty good research to support the switch.

How Did the Paleo Diet Start?

Back in the 1970s a gastroenterologist by the name of Walter L. Voegtlin observed that digestive diseases such as colitis, Crohn's disease, and irritable bowel syndrome were much more prevalent in people who followed a modern Western diet versus those whose diet consisted largely of vegetables, fruits, nuts, and lean meats. He began treating patients with these disorders by recommending diets low in carbohydrates and high in animal fats.

Unfortunately, the medical world simply wasn't ready to give up the idea that a low-fat, low-calorie diet was the healthiest way to eat, so Dr. Voegtlin's observations and research went largely unnoticed, and the Paleo diet was shoved to the back of the drawer.

The Stone Age for Modern Times

Fast-forward a decade, to a point when medical researchers had gained considerably more insight into how the human body actually works. Melvin Konner, S. Boyd Eaton, and Marjorie Shostak of Emory University published a book called *The Paleolithic Prescription: A Program of Diet & Exercise and a Design for Living*. They then followed up with a second book, *The Stone-Age Health Programme: Diet and Exercise as Nature Intended*. The first book became the foundation for most of the modern versions of the Paleo diet, while the second backed it up with more research.

The main difference between these doctors' research and Voegtlin's original work was that instead of eliminating any foods that our ancestors wouldn't have had access to, as Voegtlin did, Konner, Eaton, and Shostak encouraged eating foods that were nutritionally and proportionally similar to a traditional caveman's diet. Because it was more realistic, the diet caught on like wildfire, and the research in favor of it continues to grow to this day.

What Can You Eat?

Paleo is one of the easiest diets on the planet to follow: just remember to keep it real. If it's processed, artificial, or otherwise not directly from the earth, don't eat it. It's that simple. Dairy is one of the foods that people debate whether to allow, and it will be discussed later. But for now, consider it forbidden. Here's a list of the delicious, healthy foods that the Paleo diet allows:

- Eggs
- Healthy oils—olive and coconut are best, canola oil is currently hotly debated

- Lean animal proteins

- Nuts and seeds (note that peanuts are *not* nuts)

- Organic fruits

- Organic vegetables

- Seafood, especially cold-water fish such as salmon and tuna to get the most omega-3 fatty acids

Sounds kind of familiar, doesn't it? That's because it's probably what your doctor encouraged you to eat more of the last time that you went to see him or her. Now let's take a look at some foods that are off the table if you're going to eat Stone Age style:

- Alcohol

- Artificial foods, such as preservatives and zero-calorie sweeteners

- Cereal grains, such as wheat, barley, hops, corn, oats, rye, and rice

- Dairy (though some followers allow dairy for the health benefits)

- Legumes (including peanuts)

- Processed foods, such as wheat flour and sugar

- Processed meats, such as bacon, deli meats, sausage, and canned meats

- Starchy vegetables (although these are currently under debate)

Frequently Asked Questions

Now that you have a general idea of what you can and cannot eat, you may still have a few questions. So here's a list of those most frequently asked.

Q. Why do you have to quit drinking?

A. Beer is basically liquid grain, and it's packed with empty calories. Many types of alcoholic products contain gluten. Mixed drinks and wine are often loaded with sugar. If you absolutely can't go without that Friday-night cocktail, shoot for red wine, tequila, potato vodka, or white rum—and be careful what you mix it with.

Q. Why are legumes forbidden? They're natural foods and great sources of protein.

A. Most legumes, in their raw state, are toxic. They contain *lectins*—proteins that bind carbohydrates and have been shown to cause such autoimmune diseases as lupus and rheumatoid arthritis. The phytates in many legumes inhibit your absorption of critical minerals, and the protease inhibitors interfere with how your body breaks down protein.

Q. Why no dairy?

A. This one's under debate and there are many Paleo followers who still incorporate dairy regularly into their diets. The main reason that dairy is generally forbidden is that humans are the only animals who drink milk as adults, and many food allergies and digestive disorders are lactose related. There's a much more scientific answer for this question, but it boils down to believing or not believing that milk is bad for you.

Q. How will I lose weight while eating fat?

A. This is a question that most people have at first because we're all programmed to believe that red meat is bad for your heart.

The fact is, lean, organic, free-range meat is an excellent source of protein and many other vitamins and minerals. You're not going to be living on it alone—you're going to be incorporating it into a healthful diet.

Q. Peanuts are nuts and corn is a vegetable, so why are they off-limits?

A. Actually, peanuts are legumes and corn is a grain. Make sure you know what food groups your meals belong to, or you may sabotage your efforts to be healthier.

Bread is like dresses, hats, and shoes—
in other words, essential!

—Emily Post

6

THE BENEFITS OF PALEO

Many people turn to the Paleo diet because of the weight-loss benefits, but that's not where the idea originated. If you remember, the diet was created by a gastroenterologist to help his patients with various disorders. Of course, weight loss is a wonderful side effect that has its own set of healthy benefits.

When you add in the myriad other perks, going caveman is almost a no-brainer. Let's take a quick peek at some of the biggest health benefits of following a Paleo diet.

Weight Loss

Because this is one of the primary reasons many people decide to switch to a Paleo diet, we'll start here. Because you're eliminating empty carbs and adding in lots of healthful plant fiber and lean protein, losing weight will be much easier. A few other factors that contribute to healthy weight loss include:

- Plant fiber takes longer to digest, so you will feel full longer.

- Lean proteins help keep your energy levels steady while you build muscle.

- Omega-3s help boost your metabolism and reduce body fat.

- You will be eating a greater volume of food but taking in fewer calories.

The bottom line is you will be consuming foods that help your body function the way that it's supposed to, and one of the natural side effects of that is weight loss.

Healthy Digestive System

The theory behind the Paleo diet is that eating grains, dairy, and other foods on the excluded list can cause digestive upset, inflammation, and discomfort because our bodies aren't adapted to eating them. Also, your digestive tract needs fiber to help it sweep food through your system, otherwise it builds up and causes problems. Some of the conditions that may be improved by going caveman include:

- Colitis

- Constipation

- Gas

- Heartburn

- Irritable bowel syndrome

Many people who begin the Paleo diet for other reasons, such as weight loss or heart health, report improved digestive health. Yet another reason that this incredible diet is worth your time!

Type 2 Diabetes Prevention

Type 2 diabetes has reached disastrous proportions in the United States and other cultures that have adopted a Western diet. Historically an adult disease, children are now developing this debilitating illness at an alarming rate, and there's no sign of this trend changing. One of the main culprits is excess consumption of processed sugars and flours.

You can literally save your own life by simply eliminating these calorie-laden, low-nutrition foods from your diet. The Paleo diet helps you avoid type 2 diabetes as well as metabolic syndrome, a precursor to many different diseases, for the following reasons:

- Omega-3s help reduce belly fat, an indicator of diabetes and metabolic syndrome.

- Lean proteins and plant fiber help increase insulin resistance so that your sugar levels don't spike.

- The vitamin C that's so readily available in citrus fruits and colorful veggies helps reduce belly fat.

- Lean protein takes longer to metabolize so you avoid energy highs and lows.

Immune Health

When you eat foods that your body isn't adapted to, such as processed wheat, legumes, and dairy products, your body produces an allergic response in the form of inflammation. You may not experience any obvious outward symptoms or you could notice dark circles under your eyes as well as a feeling of general lethargy. You may attribute these symptoms to stress or exhaustion, but they could also be the sign of a chronic allergy.

Inflammation in your body is damaging if it occurs chronically, and it has been causally linked to such autoimmune disorders as:

- Fibromyalgia

- Lupus

- Multiple sclerosis

- Rheumatoid arthritis

- Several different types of cancer

Chronic inflammation can be a serious threat to your health because there are often no symptoms until you have developed a disease. Switching to the Paleo diet may help reduce or eliminate your risk for many of these types of debilitating illnesses.

Cardiovascular Health

For most of your life, you've probably been told how horrible red meat and other animal proteins are for your heart; however, recent research indicates that this is simply not true. Remember that there's a huge difference between scarfing down a fatty hamburger or sausage and enjoying a lean, organic, grass-fed steak. The burger and sausage are full of saturated fats, and in most cases, hormones and additives.

On the other hand, organic steak is a lean, nutritious protein that delivers essential vitamins and minerals with very little bad fat and no empty calories, preservatives, or hormones. When you add omega-3 fatty acid and LDL-lowering healthy fats into the mix, you've got a wonderful heart-healthy meal.

A Few Final Words on Health

The health benefits of giving up processed flour, refined sugar, and foods that cause inflammatory responses could fill an entire doctoral thesis, and the advantages to eliminating hormones and artificial additives from foods could fill another one. We didn't even touch on how a Paleo diet can help with allergies, cancer, brain health, joint health, or celiac disease, but we will cover some of these topics as we discuss the health risks of gluten in the next chapter. Suffice it to say that the benefits of going Paleo far outweigh the relatively minor inconvenience of giving up a few foods.

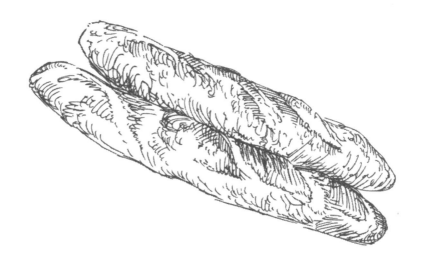

Rather a piece of bread with a happy heart than wealth with grief.

—Egyptian Proverb

7

THE TROUBLE WITH GLUTEN

We've discussed many of the health benefits of switching to a Paleo diet, but one of the main benefits is that the foods enjoyed in the Paleo diet don't have gluten in them. For millions of people worldwide, eating caveman-style is a relatively simple way to avoid digestive upset and even the cancers that are caused by an allergy to gluten.

What Is Gluten?

Latin for "glue," *gluten* is a protein found in wheat and grains that gives ground flours elasticity and helps them to rise. It's also the binding component that gives bread its chewy texture and keeps it from crumbling apart after baking. Gluten can be removed from flour because it is insoluble in water. Typically when you remove the gluten, you also lose all of the good properties that make breads and cakes what they are.

Without gluten, your baked goods won't rise and they'll have a grainy, crumbly texture. They won't taste anything like their gluten-laden cousins, and you probably won't want to eat more than the first bite. Because of an increasing demand for gluten-free products, food corporations have dedicated a tremendous amount of time and money into creating tasty, effective, gluten-free products. Unfortunately, most commercially prepared gluten-free recipe mixes still fall short.

Is the Paleo Diet Gluten-Free?

Because gluten naturally occurs in wheat and grains, the Paleo diet is completely gluten free. All grain products are strictly forbidden. Remember, the original creator of the diet was a gastroenterologist developing a plan that would help his patients with gastric disorders. Gluten intolerance is one of the most prevalent causes of gastrointestinal distress in Western civilization.

What Is Gluten Intolerance?

Gluten intolerance, or celiac disease in its advanced stage, is a condition that damages the small intestine. It is usually triggered by eating foods that have gluten in them. Some of these foods include:

- Bread

- Cookies

- Just about any baked goods

- Most flours, including white and wheat flours

- Pasta

- Pizza dough

Gluten triggers an immune response in the small intestine that causes damage to the inside of the organ. This can lead to an inability to absorb vital nutrients. Other illnesses associated with this disease include lactose intolerance, bone loss, several types of cancer, neurological complications, and malnutrition. Diseases notwithstanding, just the symptoms of gluten intolerance can disrupt daily life. They include:

- Depression

- Fatigue

- Joint pain

- Neuropathy

- Osteoporosis

- Rashes

- Severe diarrhea

- Stomach cramps

These are only a few of the symptoms that a person with gluten intolerance can suffer from, and because all foods that contain gluten are forbidden on the Paleo diet, you can see why this diet has become so popular.

The Harmful Effects of Gluten

Gluten doesn't just harm people with fully developed celiac disease. It's actually harmful to us all. Long-term studies indicate that people who have even a mild sensitivity to gluten exhibit a significantly higher risk of death than people who do not. The worst part is that 99 percent of people with gluten sensitivity don't even know they have it. They attribute their symptoms to other conditions, such as stress or fatigue.

Absorption Malfunction

One of the attributes that many obese or overweight people share is the fact that they still feel hungry after eating a full meal. This feeling of hunger is because gluten sensitivity is preventing your body from absorbing vital nutrients.

Food Addiction

Chemicals called *exorphins* in some foods cause you to crave food even when you're not hungry. Food addiction is a serious issue and doesn't necessarily denote a lack of willpower; these exorphins are actually a druglike chemical released in your brain that creates an irresistible desire for more food. Gluten contains as many as fifteen different exorphins.

Though food companies have created gluten-free foods, they often replace the gluten with flavor enhancers such as sodium and sugar, which can still seriously sabotage your dieting and fitness efforts. Another advantage to the Paleo diet is that by following it, you're not only eliminating gluten, but also avoiding the pitfalls of commercially prepared foods that continue to make you sick.

Other Conditions Related to Gluten

Numerous other conditions are related to gluten sensitivity, and many professionals postulate that this is simply because our bodies aren't adapted to eating grains and therefore your body treats them as allergens. Other symptoms or disorders linked to eating gluten include:

- Anxiety

- Autism

- Dementia

- Migraines

- Mouth sores

- Schizophrenia

- Seizures

These aren't just minor aches and pains, although gluten sensitivity can cause those, too. These are major diseases and conditions that can ruin your life. It's no wonder that people who know that they suffer from gluten intolerance consider the Paleo diet.

Health Benefits of Going Gluten Free

Obviously, there are countless benefits of giving up gluten, but here are a few that may be of particular interest to you:

- Decreased chance of several types of cancer

- Healthy, painless digestion

- Healthy skin

- Improved brain function

- Improved mood

- Reduced appetite

- Weight loss (or gain, if you're underweight because of malnutrition)

With the obvious advantages of giving up grains, it's difficult to understand exactly why people would hesitate. It's just a matter of making some adjustments to your diet, and now that knowledge about both food and health is increasing, there are some great alternatives out there that will help you get rid of your addiction to grains—including the recipes in this book!

Without bread, all is misery.

—William Cobbett

8

PALEO FOOD GUIDE

Shopping for foods that are Paleo friendly can be a daunting task when you're first starting out. What's allowed and what's not? What are all of those mystery ingredients that are listed on food labels? For the most part, stocking your refrigerator and pantry is fairly simple, but there are going to be times when you don't want to eat just steak and broccoli, and there will be other times when you need something fast and simple. Don't worry—you'll get the hang of it.

There are a few different versions of the Paleo diet, but for the sake of this discussion, we're going to take the modern middle road so that it's easier for you to make the transition to your new, healthier lifestyle. Throughout the following pages, we're going to discuss what foods are okay and where you can find them. We'll also discuss some alternate ingredients for baking bread and other goodies that won't get you kicked out of the cave!

Paleo Pantry and Kitchen Tips

The first bit of good news is that you're not going to be counting calories. Instead, you're going to try to keep your portions in line with what your ancestors most likely ate. A diet that consists of 50 to 60 percent protein, 30 to 40 percent healthy carbs, and 5 to 10 percent healthy vegetable fats such as extra-virgin olive oil, avocados, nuts, and seeds is the general goal.

Basically, when you're stacking your plate, put your protein on one side and your fruits and veggies on the other. Snacks can be whatever you want, but veggies and nuts are great choices. Be careful with nuts and fruits: they might be good for you, but they are also high in calories and can sabotage your weight-loss efforts if you're not careful.

If Possible, Go Raw

Many fruits and vegetables lose nutritional value when you cook them, so whenever possible, eat them raw. You'll also eat less because you'll be chewing more. If you opt to cook your veggies, steam them lightly so they maintain their bright colors. A key clue that you've cooked your greens to death is that they've lost that pretty vibrant green hue and turned an olive color. Try to avoid that.

Steaming, baking, grilling, and broiling are all great methods of cooking and require little added fat to prevent sticking. It should go without saying that the fryer can go in the garage to be sold at your next rummage sale.

Cooking on the Fly

Meals away from home can be a real challenge when you're first starting out. Restaurants are filled with tempting burgers and fries, and you have no idea what's in the salad dressings. If you must eat out, order a plain garden salad with oil and vinegar. You could also request a steak or chicken breast to go on top, but make sure that they either grill it dry or use olive oil.

It is better to avoid eating out at the beginning of this diet. Instead, make an amazing soup at home for dinner with enough left over that you aren't tempted to go out for a quick fix. That way, you know what's in your food, and you know that it's going to be delicious!

Planning Ahead

If you know in advance what you're going to eat for lunch or for dinner, you're not going to be as likely to cheat with something quick from the vending machine. Take snacks to work with you so that the box of doughnuts by the copy machine isn't so tempting. Here's a food list to help you get your pantry stocked up and ready to rock Stone Age style.

Meats and Proteins

Your meats need to come from grass-fed, organic livestock; free-range poultry; or wild-caught fish and seafood. Wild game is great, too, if you're so inclined. Actually, meats such as venison are extremely low in bad fats while high in good fats and lean protein, so feel free to partake!

Fruits and Vegetables

If at all possible, shop at your local farmers' market for fresh organic fruits and veggies. Because the Paleo diet is dependent upon your creativity to complete a hot, fresh, delicious meal without the aid of flours, fats, and other no-no's, you're going to have to learn a number of ways to prepare dishes. Plus, if you're offering a wide variety of foods that your family knows and loves, you won't be under so much pressure to create a single main dish that everybody will eat and enjoy.

Tomatoes are a great addition to any salad and make a flavorful base for soups and sauces. They're packed with nutrients and have so many uses that you should always have some on hand. Other staples should include carrots, peppers, cauliflower, and celery.

For fruits, opt for ones that are high in nutrients and relatively low in sugar, such as stone fruits and berries. Berries are also fabulous sources of antioxidants, phytonutrients, and vitamins. Apples are an easy grab-and-go food, as are peaches, oranges, and bananas. The dark tip of the banana that you usually pick off is rich in vitamin K, so eat it!

Oils and Fats

Oils high in saturated fats, such as corn oil and vegetable oil, are out. Opt instead for oils that are high in omega-3s such as olive, coconut, and avocado oil.

Seasonings

Your success with making the transition to the caveman way of eating is largely dependent on how flavorful your food is. As a result, you're going to need to incorporate various herbs and spices to make your dishes delicious. Here are a few that you should always have on hand:

- Allspice

- Black pepper

- Basil

- Cayenne pepper

- Cinnamon

- Cloves

- Crushed red pepper

- Curry powder

- Dry mustard

- Garlic (fresh and powdered)

- Mustard seed

- Oregano

- Paprika

- Parsley

- Rosemary

- Thyme

Finally, you'll probably want to keep some snacks on hand. Now, that does *not* mean cupcakes, potato chips, or crackers. There are, however, still many options, such as certain beef jerkies (or even better, make your own!), dried fruits, nuts, and seeds. They're satisfying and add nutrients to your diet instead of unhealthful fats.

Paleo Shopping Tips

Going to the grocery store is going to be a bit of a challenge at first, just as it is anytime you make changes to your diet. Especially if you're accustomed to eating a large amount of refined flour and sugar and aren't yet over your sugar addiction, it's not going to be easy. It's okay, though—we have a few tips to help you along your way:

- Shop for your produce at the local farmers' market, if possible.

- When at the grocery store, shop around the perimeter of the store. That's where most stores keep all of their meats and produce, and 99 percent of your food is going to come from those departments. If you need to get something from an aisle, go straight in, get it, and get back to the perimeter before those cookies catch your eye!

- Make a list and stick to it.

- If you do choose to eat canned fruits and veggies, make sure you read the label so you're not getting hidden sodium, sugar, and preservatives.

- Buy meat in bulk when you see a sale.

- Don't shop hungry! Have a low-fat, high-protein snack before you go so you aren't tempted while you're there.

Alternative Ingredients for Baking Paleo

So if you can't use flour, animal milk, or sugar, does that mean that you'll never have another sandwich or muffin? Absolutely not. Due to the massive increase in demand for gluten-free baking products, there are now several different Paleo-friendly options available to give you something to toast with your fruit in the morning. The great thing is that, unlike first-generation gluten-free flours, the latest creations are not only healthy, but delicious, too.

- Almond flour or meal—Almond flour is made from finely ground blanched almonds. Almond meal is much coarser because it is simply unblanched almonds ground up with their skins on. The flour is generally the best option for baking if you're looking for a substitute. It lends a mildly nutty flavor to your recipes.

- Coconut flour—This flour is made from coconut meat after the milk is extracted. It's extremely high in fiber and low in digestible carbs. Because it's so high in fiber, it is great as a weight-loss aid. Studies have actually shown that consuming a product with ¼ cup coconut flour can decrease caloric intake by as much as 10 percent.

- Flaxseed meal—This is a bit coarser than almond or coconut flour, so the bread texture will be significantly different unless you mix it with finer-ground flours. It lends a nutty flavor to your baked goods. The health benefits of flax are numerous: it acts as an anti-inflammatory, helps prevent heart disease, and lowers your blood pressure and cholesterol. Flax is also a fabulous source of fiber.

- Coconut oil—A wide range of health benefits is derived from coconut oil. It's good for your heart, your digestion, and your immune system, and is also useful in helping with weight loss. It has a light, but distinct coconut flavor.

- Almond butter—Almonds are high on nearly every single "world's healthiest foods" list on the planet. Almond butter gives a nice nutty flavor reminiscent of peanut butter to your dishes.

- Cashew butter—Rich in several different vitamins, cashew butter is also high in protein and is a good substitute for butter or peanut butter in a recipe. It does, of course, taste like cashews.

- Macadamia butter—Macadamia nuts are a rich source of dietary fiber and monounsaturated fats. The butter is sweet and creamy and helps reduce bad cholesterol while increasing good cholesterol. Macadamia butter is a good replacement for regular butter and has a sweet, nutty flavor.

- Almond milk—Pressed from the flesh of almonds, almond milk is high in protein and low in bad fats. It's a healthy, delicious replacement for dairy and has an extremely mild flavor that is barely noticeable.

- Coconut milk—Pressed from the meat of the coconut, coconut milk helps maintain stable blood sugar and promotes cardiovascular, bone, muscle, and nerve health. It gives a rich, sweet coconut flavor to your dishes.

All of these alternative ingredients add luscious flavors to your dishes and will really make them more multidimensional than traditional white flour and animal milk. You're also getting several nutritional benefits that you wouldn't get with old-school ingredients. By the way, honey is a Paleo-friendly ingredient that can be used sparingly as a sweetener in baked goods.

Friendship is the bread of the heart.

—Mary Russell Mitford

9

10 TIPS FOR LIVING PALEO

Just as with any change, adjusting to the Paleo diet will take you some time. After all, you're not only changing your diet, you're changing the way you think about food. Ingredients that you've known and loved for most of your life are now strictly off limits. If you're allowing yourself to have caffeine (which many Paleo dieters do not), then it's probably the only part of your morning meal that will remain the same.

Now you're going to be eating plenty of fruits, vegetables, and lean proteins, so you shouldn't ever be hungry. If you are, just eat something! You're not going to be counting calories, but you still need to be cautious about what you eat because, just as in most diets, all Paleo-approved foods are *not* equal. You're going to hit some rough spots, too, so here are some tips to get you through.

1. Go Cold Turkey

If you're serious about changing your lifestyle and want to be successful with your transition, submerge yourself in it completely. Clear all of the non-Paleo foods from your pantry and your refrigerator, and head to the grocery store. Don't buy anything that isn't on your list, and don't stop for a "final burger" on your way home.

2. Stick with It

For the first week or so, you'll probably have decreased energy because you're not eating a ton of sugar and empty carbs. Your body will have to adapt to burning proteins and complex carbs for energy. Just push through it and remember that if you do, you're going to have more energy than ever once your sugar addiction is over.

3. Think Positive

This is a positive life change, not a trip to the gallows. Don't look for ways to cheat or try to find loopholes because the only person you're cheating is yourself. If you find that the diet is too difficult to follow or if your energy levels are flagging, feed a few more carbs back into your diet and allow your body to adjust slowly.

4. Head to the Gym

There's nothing that gives you more of a sense of accomplishment than going to the gym and getting in a good workout. It has a way of making you want to eat healthful foods and take better care of yourself, so it's a great tool to help you stick with it.

5. Give It a Month

You're probably not going to be feeling so great for the first week on the diet, so that's not a good time to make a decision regarding your health. By week two, you're going to be through your detox and gaining steam, but you'll still be longingly eyeing the chips.

Give the Paleo diet a chance for a full thirty days, and if you haven't gotten the results that you were looking for, then you may consider whether or not it's right for you. But don't give up too early.

6. Don't Fear the Fat

You've most likely been told for years that fat is bad: *Avoid fat. Fat makes you fat. Fat makes you sick.* Well, some fats do, but not the healthy ones that you'll be eating on the Paleo diet. So go ahead and eat without fear. Trim extra fat off and cook using methods that allow for the most fat to cook off, but don't obsess about it; there are good fats and bad fats, and Paleo foods are generally the good kind.

7. Plan Ahead

This is probably one of the biggest keys to your success. Don't get stuck out in public with no food when hunger strikes because that will tempt you to head to those Golden Arches. Instead, prepare in advance so you have healthful meals and snacks ready to eat when you need them.

8. Transition with a Friend

As with any other diet, you'll have a better rate of success if you start with a friend. It'll be even better if you start with a spouse or significant other because he or she is right there under the same roof with you and can provide support.

9. Beware of Wolves in Sheeps' Clothing

Many foods will claim to be Paleo friendly but won't be. They'll have some kind of artificial garbage, sugar, or gluten in them that will make them inedible. If nothing else, they may contain lots of calories or forbidden oils. Just be careful and read your labels.

10. Eat What You Like

Just because you're changing the way that you eat doesn't mean you have to give up the foods that you love. Find ways to modify your favorite recipes so you're still eating foods that you enjoy.

INDEX

31462171R00092

Made in the USA
Lexington, KY
12 April 2014